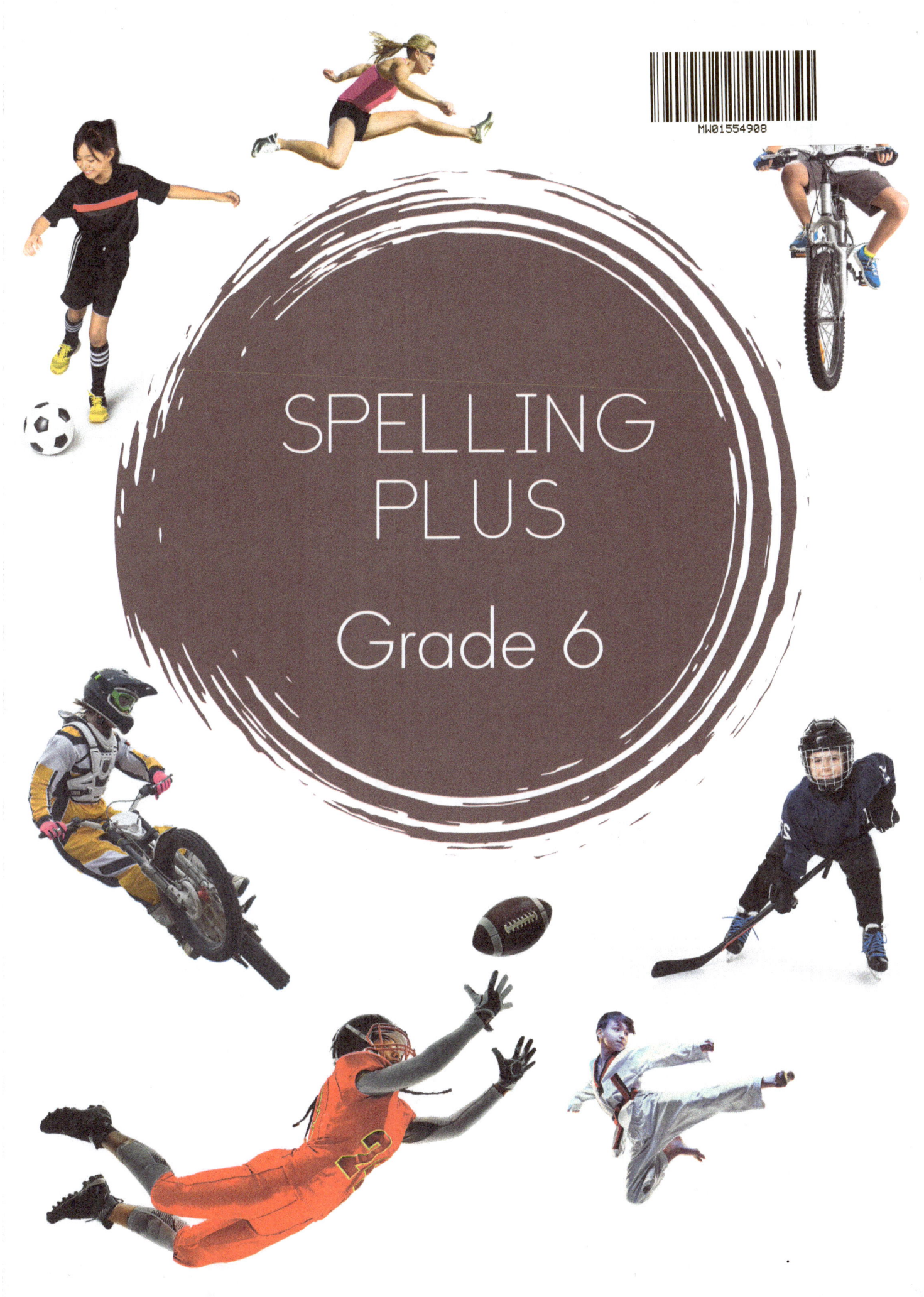

SPELLING PLUS

Grade 6

Third Edition

purposeful design publications

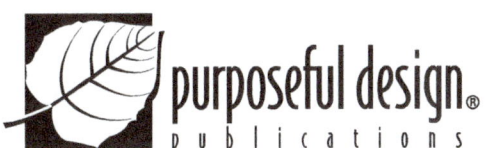

Colorado Springs, Colorado

© 1991, 2009, 2019 by Purposeful Design Publications
All rights reserved. First edition 1991.
Second Edition 2009
Third Edition 2019

No portion of this book may be reproduced, stored in a retrieval system, or transmitted, in any form or by any means—mechanical, photocopying, recording, or otherwise—without prior written permission of Purposeful Design Publications.

Purposeful Design Publications is the publishing division of the Association of Christian Schools International (ACSI) and is committed to the ministry of Christian school education, to enable Christian educators and schools worldwide to effectively prepare students for life. As the publisher of textbooks, trade books, and other educational resources within ACSI, Purposeful Design Publications strives to produce biblically sound materials that reflect Christian scholarship and stewardship and that address the identified needs of Christian schools around the world.

References to books, computer software, and other ancillary resources in this series are not endorsements by ACSI Purposeful Design Publications. These materials were selected to provide teachers with additional resources appropriate to the concepts being taught and to promote student understanding and enjoyment.

Unless otherwise identified, all Scripture quotations are taken from the Holy Bible, New King James Version (NKJV), © 1982 by Thomas Nelson, Inc. Used by permission. All rights reserved.

Photograph of Eric Liddell on Student Edition page 100 courtesy of the Liddell family.

Printed in the United States of America
25 24 23   4 5 6

Spelling Plus, Grade 6
Purposeful Design Spelling Plus series
ISBN 978-1-58331-317-6   Student Edition   Catalog #60061

Purposeful Design Publications
A Division of ACSI
PO Box 62249 • Colorado Springs, CO 80962
Customer Service: 800-367-0798 • Website: www.purposefuldesign.org

Table of Contents

Chapter 1 Short Vowels 1
Chapter 2 Long Vowels 5
Chapter 3 Words with **ei** and **ie** 9
Chapter 4 Words with **ou** 13
Chapter 5 Vowel Combinations 17
Chapter 6 Review Chapters 1–5 21
Chapter 7 Schwa **o** 25
Chapter 8 Schwa in Final Syllables 29
Chapter 9 Schwa in Unstressed Syllables 33
Chapter 10 Words with **ci**, **si**, **ti**, and **xi** 37
Chapter 11 Consonants Before **i** and **u** 41
Chapter 12 Review Chapters 7–11 45
Chapter 13 Homophones and Homographs 49
Chapter 14 Compound Words 53
Chapter 15 Endings 57
Chapter 16 Endings 61
Chapter 17 Endings 65
Chapter 18 Review Chapters 13–17 69
Chapter 19 Greek Roots 73
Chapter 20 Greek Roots 77
Chapter 21 Greek and Latin Roots 81
Chapter 22 Hard and Soft **c**, **g** 85
Chapter 23 Variant Consonant Spellings 89
Chapter 24 Review Chapters 19–23 93

Chapter 25 Prefixes 97
Chapter 26 Prefixes 101
Chapter 27 Suffixes 105
Chapter 28 Suffixes 109
Chapter 29 R-Controlled Vowels 113
Chapter 30 Review Chapters 25–29 117
Chapter 31 Frequently Misspelled Words 121
Chapter 32 Words from French and Italian 125
Chapter 33 Words from Spanish 129
Chapter 34 Words from German 133
Chapter 35 Words from Asian Languages 137
Chapter 36 Review Chapters 31–35 141

Student Resources

Word Bank 145
Pronunciation Key 154
Spelling Dictionary 155

Name _____

Review Chapters 1–5
Chapter 1

Pattern Words

Chapter 1	Chapter 2	Chapter 3	Chapter 4	Chapter 5
Short Vowels	Long Vowels	Words with ei and ie	Words with ou	Vowel Combinations
insist	unify	seize	route	decoy
hiccup	visor	grief	couple	neutral
difficult	basis	weird	sought	euphoric
contact	ideally	leisure	though	moisture
subtotal	closely	receipt	poultry	awkward
method	rotation	conceit	drought	awesome
attitude	medium	disbelief	encounter	beautifully
function	reasons	received	thoroughly	exhausted
progress	highlights	believers	resounding	precaution
anticipate	numerical	lieutenant	throughout	renewable
benefitted	daydream	sovereign	thoughtlessly	newsworthy
technology	cooperate	foreigner	announcements	unauthorized

Content Words

circuit	agile	axles	slalom	rappel
engine	hybrid	traction	designs	fissures
terrain	cycling	flexibility	facilitate	anchored
physical	helmet	technique	freestyle	ascending
simulated	designed	composite	fasteners	bouldering
equipment	diameter	maneuvers	popularity	formations
dangerous	motocross	competitive	extraordinary	outcroppings

Vocabulary Words

final	deflect	adjoining	eclectic	errant
finalist	reflective	rejoined	selection	error
reversed	aspiration	inquire	inspection	describing
traversed	perspire	inquiry	respected	indescribable

Read Chapter 1 Pattern Words. Follow the directions given.

1. Make a check next to the words with the **short a** sound in the first syllable.

2. Circle the words with the **short e** sound in the first syllable.

3. Underline the words with the **short i** sound in the first syllable.

4. Box the words with the **short o** sound in the first syllable.

5. Make a star next to the words with the **short u** sound in the first syllable.

Find a word that fits each clue. Write each letter in a box.

6.2

Review Chapters 1–5
Chapters 2–3

Across
1. in close proximity
2. the upper, front piece of a helmet
3. a turn around an axis
4. relating to numbers

Down
1. to collaborate
5. the foundation
6. average; intermediate
7. to unite

unify
visor
basis
ideally
closely
rotation
medium
reasons
highlights
numerical
daydream
cooperate

Read each word. Decide if it is spelled correctly or incorrectly. Fill in the circle. Write each word correctly.

Correct   Incorrect

seize
grief
weird
leisure
receipt
conceit
disbelief
received
believers
lieutenant
sovereign
foreigner

8. leiutenant ○ ○ _____
9. sieze ○ ○ _____
10. foreigner ○ ○ _____
11. wierd ○ ○ _____
12. disbeleif ○ ○ _____
13. liesure ○ ○ _____
14. soveriegn ○ ○ _____
15. reciept ○ ○ _____
16. grief ○ ○ _____
17. conciet ○ ○ _____
18. received ○ ○ _____
19. beleivers ○ ○ _____

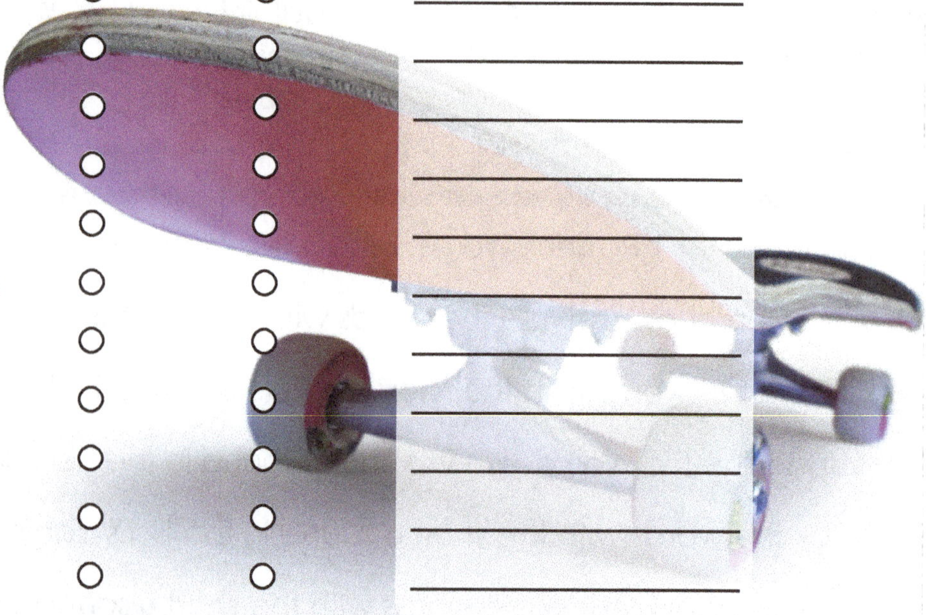

22

Name _____

6.3

Find the words in the word search. Circle them and write them on the lines. The words go across, down, diagonally, and backwards. Some of the words share letters.

Review Chapters 1–5
Chapters 4–5

```
a n n o u n c e m e n t s y h o
s t h o r o u g h l y z l g g u
o o e l e x p o u l t r y i u g
u d j t r v w e l p u o c o o h
g x u o d r o u g h t b j f h t
h o u k t h r o u g h o u t t n
t t h o u g h t l e s s l y s p
e b y x r e t n u o c n e y e r
g n r e s o u n d i n g v l l v
```

route
couple
sought
though
poultry
drought
encounter
thoroughly
resounding
throughout
thoughtlessly
announcements

_____ _____ _____
_____ _____ _____
_____ _____ _____
_____ _____ _____

Unscramble each word and write it correctly.

decoy
neutral
euphoric
moisture
awkward
awesome
beautifully
exhausted
precaution
renewable
newsworthy
unauthorized

1. z e d n u a o r i u t h _____
2. w s w n h y r e o t _____
3. a u e p r t i o c n _____
4. w a b r e e l e n _____
5. w k a a r w d _____
6. o c y d e _____
7. u t r a l n e _____
8. p e u o r i c h _____
9. u f e l y u a b t i l _____
10. s u r m t e o i _____

6.4 Review Chapters 1–5
Content and Vocabulary Words

Read the paragraph. Write a Content Word in each shape box.

Extraordinary Sports

Extreme sports are truly ⬚⬚⬚⬚⬚⬚⬚⬚⬚⬚⬚⬚⬚ sports because they require an athlete to use ⬚⬚⬚⬚⬚⬚⬚⬚ skill in ⬚⬚⬚⬚⬚⬚⬚⬚⬚ situations. There has been a recent surge in the ⬚⬚⬚⬚⬚⬚⬚⬚⬚ of extreme sports, including motocross, ⬚⬚⬚⬚⬚⬚⬚ with BMX bikes, in-line skating and skateboarding, ⬚⬚⬚⬚⬚⬚⬚⬚⬚ snowboarding, skiing, and rock climbing. Participants need to wear safety equipment such as a ⬚⬚⬚⬚⬚⬚. Learning the proper ⬚⬚⬚⬚⬚⬚⬚⬚⬚ for any sport will minimize risk and provide for maximum enjoyment.

Word bank:
terrain
physical
dangerous
cycling
helmet
designed
traction
flexibility
technique
freestyle
popularity
extraordinary
anchored
ascending
formations

Vocabulary list:
final
finalist
traversed
deflect
reflective
aspiration
rejoined
inquire
inquiry
eclectic
selection
inspection
errant
describing
indescribable

	A	B	C	D	E	F	G	H
1	re-	se-	fin	quir	err	flect	-y	-ed
2	tra-	de	scrib	lect	join	-ing	-ive	-ation
3	in-	a-	spir	vers	spect	-able	al	-ant

Find the coordinates given. Write the Vocabulary Words.

1. B3 + C3 + H2 = _____
2. A1 + E2 + H1 = _____
3. A3 + D1 + G1 = _____
4. A1 + F1 + G2 = _____
5. C1 + G3 = _____
6. E1 + H3 = _____
7. B2 + C2 + F2 = _____
8. A3 + B2 + C2 + F3 = _____

Name _____

7.2 Word Analysis
Schwa o

Pattern Words
- collide
- eloquent
- recollect
- collegiate
- concludes
- accolades
- configured
- committee
- community
- unconvinced
- recommend
- development

The **schwa** is a vowel sound identical to **short u**.
The symbol **ə** represents the **schwa**.

Write Pattern Words to complete the exercises. Sort the schwa **o** words.

1.–6. Words with schwa **o** in the first syllable
7.–11. Words with schwa **o** in the second syllable
12. Word with schwa **o** in the third syllable

1. _____   2. _____
3. _____   4. _____
5. _____   6. _____
7. _____   8. _____
9. _____   10. _____
11. _____   12. _____

Write Content Words to complete the exercises.

13. Each football team fields eleven players at a time; the major offensive player is the q_____.
14. A s_____ is a practice game.
15. Six points are scored for a t_____.
16. The quarterback passes the ball to an offensive receiver, but a defender can catch it for an i_____.
17. Defenders must be careful not to cause i_____ when a receiver is trying to catch a pass. Interference is one of the p_____ that can be charged during the game.
18. Football teams will compete for the c_____.

Content Words
- penalties
- touchdown
- scrimmage
- interception
- interference
- quarterback
- championship

Vocabulary Words
- dominate
- dominion
- opposite
- reposition

Challenge Words
_____
_____

football

© Spelling Plus Grade 6   25

Prefix		Root		Suffix	
op-	against	domin	master	-ate	to act
re-	again	posit	place	-ion	state

7.2
Vocabulary
Schwa o

Write the Vocabulary Words.

1. _____ 2. _____
3. _____ 4. _____

Refer to the table to complete the exercises. Write the word that is being defined.

5. the state of supreme authority _____
6. something opposed or against another specified thing _____
7. to be the master over something or someone _____
8. to change the place of an item _____

Write Vocabulary Words to complete the sentence.

9. The Tigers sought to _____ the Bears on the football field.
10. The Bears took the _____ position on the field and were ready to receive the kickoff.
11. The kicker was so nervous that he had to _____ the football on the tee.
12. The crowd was tense because this game would decide which team would have _____ over all the other teams.

Choose the word that matches each definition.

13. to remember
    ○ committee   ○ recollect   ○ eloquent
14. to crash
    ○ collegiate   ○ concludes   ○ collide
15. to advise favorably
    ○ recommend   ○ development   ○ penalties
16. set up in a particular way
    ○ unconvinced   ○ community   ○ configured

Pattern Words
collide
eloquent
recollect
collegiate
concludes
accolades
configured
committee
community
unconvinced
recommend
development

Content Words
penalties
touchdown
scrimmage
interception
interference
quarterback
championship

Vocabulary Words
dominate
dominion
opposite
reposition

26

Name _____

7.3

Word Study Strategies
Schwa o

Write each list word from the pronunciation shown.

1. /kə ˈlīd/ _____
2. /ˈe lə kwənt/ _____
3. /ˈkwôr tûr bak/ _____
4. /kən ˈklo͞odz/ _____
5. /də ˈmi nyən/ _____
6. /ˈo pə zət/ _____
7. /di ˈve ləp mənt/ _____
8. /ke ˈmyo͞o nə tē/ _____
9. /ˈa kə lādz/ _____
10. /kə ˈmi tē/ _____

Pattern Words
collide
eloquent
recollect
collegiate
concludes
accolades
configured
committee
community
unconvinced
recommend
development

A <mark>compound subject</mark> is made up of two or more subjects that share the same predicate.

Write the compound subject in each sentence. Then write each simple subject. The first one is done for you.

11. The quarterback and the wide receiver connected to complete the pass.
    ___The quarterback and the wide receiver___
    ___quarterback___   ___receiver___

12. The community and the athletic committee wanted a new football stadium.
    _____
    _____ _____

13. A touchdown or an interception would give the team an advantage.
    _____
    _____ _____

14. Penalties and an interference stalled the drive to the goal line.
    _____
    _____ _____

15. The fans' accolades and the championship belonged to the Tigers.
    _____
    _____ _____

Content Words
penalties
touchdown
scrimmage
interception
interference
quarterback
championship

Vocabulary Words
dominate
dominion
opposite
reposition

I press toward the goal for the prize of the upward call of God in Christ Jesus. Philippians 3:14

© Spelling Plus Grade 6   27

EAGLES WIN!

It is almost impossible to describe the excitement at yesterday's play-off football game! The undefeated Eagles took on last year's bowl winners, the Rams. This game was for the **1**. It would prove which team had **2** over all the other teams in the football conference.

The Rams' **3** called several exciting plays that he and the coach had **4** on a chalkboard and practiced during a **5** before the game. An injury occurred when an offensive player happened to **6** with a defender. Then the quarterback threw a long pass that was intended for a receiver downfield. A defender got in the way, and a penalty was called for **7**. The quarterback threw another long pass on the next play, but it was caught by the defending team for an **8**! The Rams' offense looked very disappointed as the defense took the field. The Eagles' offense began to **9** the Rams' defense and soon the Eagles had scored the first **10**. The cheering, yelling, and other **11** of the fans were deafening! It appeared that the Eagles would have an easy win, but in the next quarter they had a number of costly **12** that kept them from scoring.

The game was tied at the beginning of the fourth quarter. The fans were **13** that the undefeated Eagles would win to continue their record. The Rams' offense looked very good. They ran the first play from the five-yard line all the way to the five-yard line on the **14** end of the field and scored on the next play. Yet, it was the Eagles who proved that they could fight back by scoring the next two touchdowns to win the game. It seemed as if the entire **15** ran down onto the field to congratulate the coach and players. What a thrilling event!

Pattern Words
collide
eloquent
recollect
collegiate
concludes
accolades
configured
committee
community
unconvinced
recommend
development

Content Words
penalties
touchdown
scrimmage
interception
interference
quarterback
championship

Vocabulary Words
dominate
dominion
opposite
reposition

1. championship
2. dominion
3. quarterback
4. configured
5. scrimmage
6. collide
7. interference
8. interception
9. dominate
10. touchdown
11. accolades
12. penalties
13. unconvinced
14. opposite
15. community

Name _____

8.2
Word Analysis
Schwa in Final Syllables

Pattern Words
- trivia
- status
- bulletin
- channel
- random
- raucous
- versatile
- broaden
- obstinate
- intramural
- momentous
- accustomed

Content Words
- league
- athlete
- statistics
- amateur
- spectator
- outfielders
- concessions

Vocabulary Words
- grateful
- gratify
- inspire
- inspiring

The **schwa** is a vowel sound identical to **short u**. The symbol ə represents the **schwa**.

Write Pattern Words to complete the exercises. Sort the words by the vowel spelling of the schwa in the final syllable.

1.–3. **a**   4.–5. **e**   6.–7. **i**
8.–9. **ou**   10.–11. **o**   12. **u**

1. _____   2. _____
3. _____   4. _____
5. _____   6. _____
7. _____   8. _____
9. _____   10. _____
11. _____   12. _____

Write Content Words to complete the exercises.

13. Every professional baseball player was once an a_____ player.

14. The Colorado Rockies and the San Diego Padres baseball teams are in the same l_____.

15. Do you know an a_____ who plays baseball or softball?

16. In baseball, the players in positions seven, eight, and nine are the o_____.

17. Most ballparks have c_____ that sell food, drinks, and memorabilia.

18. Baseball cards contain a player's s_____.

19. A home run is sometimes caught by a s_____.

Challenge Words

baseball

8.2 Vocabulary: Schwa in Final Syllables

Prefix		Root		Suffix	
in-	in	grat	thankful, pleasing	-ful	full of
		spir	breathe	-ify	to make
				-ing	continuous action

Write the Vocabulary Words.

1. _____
2. _____
3. _____
4. _____

Refer to the table to complete the exercises. Match each word to its definition.

____ 5. inspiring — a. to have a positive influence in someone's life
____ 6. grateful — b. to do something that makes someone pleased
____ 7. inspire — c. full of thanks; thankful
____ 8. gratify — d. having a continuously motivating influence on someone

Write Vocabulary Words to complete the sentence.

9. The story of how Babe Ruth overcame a difficult childhood to become one of the greatest baseball players in history is _____.

10. Do stories of how people overcome difficult situations _____ you?

11. When the team was recognized for its sportmanship, the prized trophy did _____ the coach.

12. The coach is _____ for each player on his team

Choose the word that matches each definition.

13. stubborn
    ○ random
    ○ obstinate
    ○ intramural

14. to widen
    ○ broaden
    ○ channel
    ○ raucous

15. usual
    ○ accustomed
    ○ amateur
    ○ bulletin

16. important
    ○ versatile
    ○ trivia
    ○ momentous

Pattern Words
trivia
status
bulletin
channel
random
raucous
versatile
broaden
obstinate
intramural
momentous
accustomed

Content Words
league
athlete
statistics
amateur
spectator
outfielders
concessions

Vocabulary Words
grateful
gratify
inspire
inspiring

Name _____

8.3

An inference is a conclusion reached by looking at facts. Look at the facts given in each sentence to infer the missing list word. Write the list word.

Word Study Strategies
Schwa in Final Syllables

1. Jessica is able to play several softball positions very well. She is a _____ player.
2. Tawnie, Sarah, and Lisa each have the ability to throw the ball from the outfield to the infield during a game. They are the _____.
3. Terry just joined the baseball team and does not have much experience. He is an _____ player.
4. Winning the World Series is a dream of every baseball team. Receiving the top trophy is a _____ occasion.
5. Max and his team are undefeated. They are _____ to winning.
6. Coaches encourage their team to do well. Their pep talks are motivating and _____ to the team.

Alliteration is a repetition of initial consonant sounds of several consecutive words in a phrase and is used by authors to add auditory interest to their writing.
Write a word with a repeated initial consonant sound to complete each sentence.

7. Tracie tried to trick Troy with _____ questions.
8. Connie coughed and could not drink coffee from the _____.
9. Before baseball season begins, workmen will _____ the boulevard.
10. The Lions' lineup lacks left-handers in their _____.
11. Chase chews chips while watching the sports _____.
12. On Saturdays, Seth sees the _____ of several sports teams.
13. The _____ saw the softball soar south.
14. Grady is _____ that he grabbed the ground ball.

Pattern Words
trivia
status
bulletin
channel
random
raucous
versatile
broaden
obstinate
intramural
momentous
accustomed

Content Words
league
athlete
statistics
amateur
spectator
outfielders
concessions

Vocabulary Words
grateful
gratify
inspire
inspiring

Read the paragraphs about baseball and softball. Underline the list words.

8.4

Writing Schwa in Final Syllables

Baseball and Softball

Baseball is a game that is played all over the world. It was first played in the United States in the early 1800s by children and amateur players. By the late 1800s, it developed into a professional, competitive sport played by teams in a league. A regulation baseball measures about 9 inches in circumference. A bat cannot be more than 42 inches in length. The pitcher stands 60.5 feet away from home plate and puts the ball in motion by throwing it overhand, often as fast as 90 to 100 miles per hour. The distance between each base is 90 feet. More than one talented athlete fills positions consisting of infielders and outfielders for a total of 9 players. Athletes with the best statistics in pitching, hitting, and fielding receive awards at the end of the season. The awards, such as the Cy Young Award for pitching, are named after former famous baseball athletes. The stories of former baseball players who achieved success are inspiring.

Softball is a game that is very similar to baseball, but it differs in equipment, pitching, and field size. There are three classifications to the game—slow-pitch, fast-pitch, and modified-pitch. The softball itself varies in size from 12 to 16 inches in circumference. The larger ball is used for slow-pitch while the smaller ball is used for fast-pitch. A bat cannot be more than 34 inches long. Depending on the style of softball being played, the pitcher stands 40 to 50 feet away from home plate and the bases are 60 to 65 feet apart. The ball is put into motion by an underhand pitch. In slow-pitch, a tenth player is added to the outfield. Like baseball, softball is also a worldwide sport that attracts many fans. Softball was invented in the United States in the late 1800s as an indoor sport and later as an outdoor sport. It is played as an intramural as well as an intercollegiate sport. There are also professional softball teams. A spectator can view the sport on a sports channel or at a stadium where he or she can buy refreshments from the concessions.

Pattern Words
trivia
status
bulletin
channel
random
raucous
versatile
broaden
obstinate
intramural
momentous
accustomed

Content Words
league
athlete
statistics
amateur
spectator
outfielders
concessions

Vocabulary Words
grateful
gratify
inspire
inspiring

Write complete sentences to compare and contrast the sports of baseball and softball. Use several list words.

1. What are three ways the two sports are similar? _____
   _____
   _____

2. What are three ways the two sports are different? _____
   _____
   _____
   _____
   _____

32

Name _____

9.2

Word Analysis
Schwa in Unstressed Syllables

Pattern Words

imitate
aghast
charity
satellite
algebra
apology
qualified
pedestal
diagram
individual
celebrate
antiquated

A **schwa** is a vowel sound identical to **short u**. The symbol **ə** represents the **schwa**. Schwas often occur in unstressed syllables.

An <mark>unstressed syllable</mark> is a syllable that is pronounced with less emphasis than the stressed syllable in the word. There is no accent mark on an unstressed syllable.

Read the pronunciation of each word. Circle the letter or letters in each word that makes the schwa sound.

1. /ə 'gast/ aghast
2. /'al jə brə/ algebra
3. /'an tə kwā təd/ antiquated
4. /ə 'po lə jē/ apology
5. /'se lə brāt/ celebrate
6. /'chär ə tē/ charity
7. /'dī ə gram/ diagram
8. /'i mə tāt/ imitate
9. /in də 'vi jə wəl/ individual
10. /'pe dəs təl/ pedestal
11. /'kwä lə fīd/ qualified
12. /'sa tə līt/ satellite

Write Content Words to complete the exercises.

13. The governing body of worldwide soccer is the *Federation Internationale de Football* A_____.
14. The defender, midfielder, attacker, and g_____ are the four main positions in soccer.
15. Midfielders, or halfbacks, must be proficient in skills of d_____ and o_____.
16. On a soccer team, forwards, or attackers, are also known as s_____ and are responsible for scoring goals.
17. There is only one r_____ in soccer.
18. The World Cup t_____ is considered the most popular spectator event in the world.

Content Words

offense
defense
strikers
referee
association
goalkeeper
tournament

Vocabulary Words

bilingual
linguistics
exposure
impose

Challenge Words

_____
_____

soccer

9.2
Vocabulary — Schwa in Unstressed Syllables

Prefix		Root		Suffix	
bi-	two	lingu	tongue	-al	related to
ex-	out of	quir	put	-ist	one who
im-	into			-ics	related to
				-ure	process

Write the Vocabulary Words.

1. _____
2. _____
3. _____
4. _____

Refer to the table to complete the exercises. Write the word that is being defined.

5. the process of being made known _____
6. related to speaking two languages _____
7. related to the study of language _____
8. to put down, insist upon, or enforce _____

Write Vocabulary Words to complete the sentences.

9. Modern technology, such as satellites, in the television industry has benefitted the worldwide _____ of soccer.
10. A referee can _____ a penalty by sometimes awarding a free kick to the opposing team.
11. A referee or the team players do not have to be _____ to understand the enforcement of fouls in soccer—a yellow card is shown for an official caution and a red card is shown for an automatic ejection.
12. Because of this worldwide yellow and red card system, a spectator does not have to be proficient in _____ to understand the rules of soccer.

Choose the word that matches each definition.

13. to cause to be old or outdated
    ○ apology   ○ association   ○ antiquated
14. a series of games
    ○ defense   ○ tournament   ○ qualified

Pattern Words
imitate
aghast
charity
satellite
algebra
apology
qualified
pedestal
diagram
individual
celebrate
antiquated

Content Words
offense
defense
strikers
referee
association
goalkeeper
tournament

Vocabulary Words
bilingual
linguistics
exposure
impose

Name _____

9.3

Word Study Strategies
Schwa in Unstressed Syllables

Use the Spelling Dictionary to answer each question.
1. What is the pronunciation for **tournament**? _____
2. What is the part of speech for **antiquated**? _____
3. What is the definition for **offense**? _____
   _____
4. What is the sample sentence for **referee**? _____
   _____
5. What is the pronunciation for **association**? _____
6. What is the part of speech for **bilingual**? _____
7. What are the definitions for **qualified**? _____
   _____
8. What is the sample sentence for **apology**? _____
   _____

Pattern Words
imitate
aghast
charity
satellite
algebra
apology
qualified
pedestal
diagram
individual
celebrate
antiquated

A compound predicate is made up of two or more predicates that share the same subject.

Write the compound predicate in each sentence. Then write each simple predicate. The first one is done for you.

9. The referee did impose his opinion and qualified for the job.
   did impose his opinion and qualified for the job
   ___did impose___   ___qualified___

10. Many soccer fans will imitate one another and celebrate a victory.
    _____
    _____   _____

11. The new tournament rules antiquated the old rules and qualified many guidelines.
    _____
    _____   _____

12. The soccer association should imitate the new guidelines and impose the latest policies.
    _____
    _____   _____

Content Words
offense
defense
strikers
referee
association
goalkeeper
tournament

Vocabulary Words
bilingual
linguistics
exposure
impose

Spelling Plus Grade 6   35

A run-on sentence is an incorrect combination of two or more complete sentences. Revise the descriptive action story about a soccer tournament using proofreading marks. Correctly write the misspelled words.

9.4

Writing
Schwa in Unstressed Syllables

Soccer Shenanigans

The crowd was eerily silent a stillness flooded the stadium as the gaolkeeper lay motionless on the field seconds earlier, the spectators had been agast when the flagrant foul was committed by a member of the the ofense.

The fast-paced, free-flowing game was full of excitement. A player on the Offense was displaying amazing promise. As he he approached the goal, he kicked the ball but continued his momentum into the Penalty area. The crowd could hear the intensity of the subsequent collision. Both players fell heavily to the ground, and silence spread throughout the stadium. The referree showed a red penalty card and did impoze a penalty on the aggressive player when he came to. He was immediately ejected from the game for his Violent behavior.

The goalkeeper stirred and the crowd roared. As he sat up, both teams rallied around him. A coach from the opposing team gave the assurance that an apolagy would be made from from the player who charged goalkeeper.

Proofreading Marks
- ◯ Circle misspellings.
- ≡ Make a capital letter.
- ⊙ Add a period.
- ⌇ Delete.
- ∧ Add something.
- / Make a small letter.
- ¶ Make a new paragraph.

Pattern Words
imitate
aghast
charity
satellite
algebra
apology
qualified
pedestal
diagram
individual
celebrate
antiquated

Content Words
offense
defense
strikers
referee
association
goalkeeper
tournament

Vocabulary Words
bilingual
linguistics
exposure
impose

1. _____   2. _____
3. _____   4. _____
5. _____   6. _____

Beloved, do not imitate what is evil, but what is good. 3 John 11

Locate the run-on sentence in the descriptive action story above. Rewrite the run-on sentence as three complete sentences.

7. _____
8. _____
9. _____

Name _____

10.2
Word Analysis
Words with ci, si, ti, and xi

Pattern Words
- anxious
- potential
- essential
- explosion
- sufficient
- beneficial
- especially
- distinction
- discussion
- obnoxious
- omniscient
- transitional

The letters **ci**, **si**, **ti**, and **xi** spell the /sh/ or /zh/ sound.

Write Pattern Words to complete the exercises.
Sort the words according to their spelling.

| 1.–4. **ci** | 5.–6. **si** | 7.–10. **ti** | 11.–12. **xi** |

1. _____   2. _____
3. _____   4. _____
5. _____   6. _____
7. _____   8. _____
9. _____   10. _____
11. _____ 12. _____

Write Content Words to complete the exercises.

13. Basketball is a sport played outdoors and in a _____ around the world.

14. To start a game, an o_____ tosses the ball into the air between two o_____ who jump to gain p_____ of the ball for their team.

15. Basketball is a game involving not only quick thinking, but also s_____.

16. Taller players have an advantage in basketball. Because of their h_____, they can shoot the ball over other players.

17. Players must be careful not to incur a t_____ foul for poor sportsmanship on the court.

Content Words
- height
- official
- arenas
- technical
- strategy
- opponents
- possession

Vocabulary Words
- immigrant
- migrate
- disrespectful
- respectable

Challenge Words
_____
_____

basketball

10.2
Vocabulary — Words with ci, si, ti, and xi

Prefix		Root		Suffix	
im-	into	migr	move	-ant	one who
dis-	not	spect	view	-ate	to act
re-	back			-ful	full of
				-able	capable of

Pattern Words
anxious
potential
essential
explosion
sufficient
beneficial
especially
distinction
discussion
obnoxious
omniscient
transitional

Content Words
height
official
arenas
technical
strategy
opponents
possession

Vocabulary Words
immigrant
migrate
disrespectful
respectable

Write the Vocabulary Words.

1. _____
2. _____
3. _____
4. _____

Refer to the table to complete the exercises. Match each word to its definition.

_____ 5. immigrant   a. not showing proper honor
_____ 6. migrate   b. capable of being viewed favorably
_____ 7. disrespectful   c. to move from one country to another
_____ 8. respectable   d. one who has moved from one country to another

Write Vocabulary Words to complete the sentences.

9. When Sasha was eleven, his parents decided to _____ from Russia to the United States.

10. Because he was a new _____, Sasha did not yet speak English.

11. Sasha saw a group of basketball players on a court near his new home. He did not want to be _____ and interrupt a game, but he wanted to participate.

12. Sasha brought a basketball and acted in a _____ manner. Soon he was invited to play.

Choose the best meaning for each underlined word. Use the Spelling Dictionary.

13. The <u>obnoxious</u> fan kept yelling at the official.
    ○ lacking in distinction   ○ showing good sportsmanship
    ○ rudely annoying   ○ considerate

14. The coach provided <u>sufficient</u> practice for all the players.
    ○ potential   ○ inspiring
    ○ grateful   ○ enough

Name _____

10.3

Word Study Strategies
Words with ci, si, ti, and xi

Write Pattern Words to complete each riddle.
1. This **ci** word is all-knowing. _____
2. This **xi** word is worried. _____
3. This **ti** word is absolutely necessary. _____
4. This **ci** word is enough. _____
5. This **ti** word stands out from others. _____
6. This **xi** word is rudely annoying. _____
7. This **ti** word shows great promise. _____
8. This **si** word is a sudden, powerful burst. _____

Write a list word that is a related form of each group of words.
9. technicality, technique, technician, _____
10. discuss, discussed, discussing, _____
11. transition, transitory, transitioned, _____
12. noxious, obnoxiously, obnoxiousness, _____
13. distinct, indistinct, distinctive, _____

Use the meaning of each related form to write a list word.
14. A **stratagem** is a clever plan for outwitting an enemy.
    To **strategize** is to devise a plan of action.
    A _____ is a careful plan or method.
15. An **office** is a special duty or position.
    Something **unofficial** does not have an authorized position or duty.
    An _____ is one whose duty is to act as a referee.
16. A **benefit** is something that promotes well-being.
    A **beneficiary** is someone who receives a benefit.
    Something _____ is that which improves one's well-being.

Pattern Words
anxious
potential
essential
explosion
sufficient
beneficial
especially
distinction
discussion
obnoxious
omniscient
transitional

Content Words
height
official
arenas
technical
strategy
opponents
possession

Vocabulary Words
immigrant
migrate
disrespectful
respectable

© Spelling Plus Grade 6

In this dialogue, Manuel describes the sport of wheelchair basketball to his friend Jamie. Read the dialogue. Write the word that matches each underlined pronunciation.

10.4

Writing
Words with ci, si, ti, and xi

Dialogue About Wheelchair Basketball

MANUEL: Hi, Jamie. Will you come with me to an /is 'pesh lē/ ₁ interesting Paralympic sporting event, a wheelchair basketball game? Before we go, we can have a /di 'sku shən/ ₂ about the game.

JAMIE: Manuel, I really want to go, but I do not know anything about wheelchair basketball. How is it played?

MANUEL: Wheelchair basketball is played by two teams of five players each. The aim of each team is to score points against the /ə 'pō nənts/ ₃ by making baskets and to prevent the other team from gaining /pə 'ze shən/ ₄ of the ball.

JAMIE: Is there any /di 'stingk shən/ ₅ between the court used in wheelchair basketball and regular basketball? Are the rules the same?

MANUEL: Wheelchair basketball is challenging because it is played on a regulation-size court and the baskets are at the same /'hīt/ ₆. The only difference in the rules is that players can move their wheels just twice in succession before they have to dribble once.

JAMIE: It sounds like fun! I do not mean to be /dis ri 'spekt fəl/ ₇, but is it /i 'sent shəl/ ₈ to be disabled to play? Do you think I could play?

MANUEL: International competition is only for athletes who have limited functional abilities. There is a /'tek ni kəl/ ₉ method used to rank each player's level of ability. You may not be able to play, but you can enjoy watching the game.

JAMIE: Let's get going!

Pattern Words
anxious
potential
essential
explosion
sufficient
beneficial
especially
distinction
discussion
obnoxious
omniscient
transitional

Content Words
height
official
arenas
technical
strategy
opponents
possession

Vocabulary Words
immigrant
migrate
disrespectful
respectable

1. _____ 2. _____ 3. _____
4. _____ 5. _____ 6. _____
7. _____ 8. _____ 9. _____

Name _____

11.2
Word Analysis
Consonants Before i and u

Pattern Words
senior
casual
cordial
brilliant
familiar
behavior
gradually
schedules
persuade
millionaire
procedure
companion

Content Words
spherical
separated
succession
endurance
gymnasium
rectangular
cooperation

Vocabulary Words
capitalism
capitalize
description
subscription

Write Pattern Words to complete the exercises.
Sort the words with consonants before **i** and **u**.

1.–6. Words with **li**, **ni**, or **vi** pronounced /y/
7.–10 Words with **di** or **du** pronounced /j/
11. Word with **su** pronounced /sw/
12. Word with **su** pronounced /zh/

1. _____ 2. _____
3. _____ 4. _____
5. _____ 6. _____
7. _____ 8. _____
9. _____ 10. _____
11. _____ 12. _____

Write Content Words to complete the exercises.

13. Volleyball is a popular team sport that is played by hitting an inflated, s_____ ball back and forth over a net. A player is not allowed to hit the ball in s_____.

14. The two categories of play that volleyball can be s_____ into are indoor play and outdoor play.

15. Indoor play usually takes place inside a g_____ and consists of six players on a team. Outdoor play is on a sand court with a team of two players. Both play situations occur on a r_____ court and require team c_____.

16. Volleyball players need to have high levels of strength and e_____.

Challenge Words
_____
_____

volleyball

Prefix		Root		Suffix	
de-	thoroughly	capit	head	-al	related to
sub-	under	script	write	-ism	condition of
				-ize	to make
				-ion	state of

11.2

Vocabulary
Consonants
Before i and u

Pattern Words
senior
casual
cordial
brilliant
familiar
behavior
gradually
schedules
persuade
millionaire
procedure
companion

Content Words
spherical
separated
succession
endurance
gymnasium
rectangular
cooperation

Vocabulary Words
capitalism
capitalize
description
subscription

Write the Vocabulary Words.

1. _____ 2. _____
3. _____ 4. _____

Refer to the table to complete the exercises. Write the word that is being defined.

5. the state or process of explanation _____
6. the condition of a free-market, economic system _____
7. the state of agreement to sign for something and pay for it _____
8. to make a profit or benefit by turning something to an advantage _____

Write Vocabulary Words to complete the sentences.

9. The television announcer gave a detailed, play-by-play _____ of the entire volleyball match.
10. A volleyball player can _____ on an opponent's mistake.
11. Wayne sent in his _____ for a new volleyball sport magazine.
12. In the economic system of _____, many professional athletes are able to market themselves and profit from their status.

Choose the word that matches each definition.

13. a sequence
    ○ companion   ○ familiar   ○ succession
14. sincere; friendly
    ○ separated   ○ cordial   ○ spherical

42

Name _____

11.3

Word Study Strategies
Consonants
Before i and u

Write a list word that belongs in each category.

1. plans, lists, agendas, _____
2. profit, benefit, gain, _____
3. conduct, actions, deeds, _____
4. higher, leading, superior, _____
5. round, circular, globular, _____
6. influence, convince, sway, _____
7. stamina, strength, fortitude, _____
8. explanation, account, report, _____
9. pleasant, friendly, respectful, _____
10. slowly, progressively, steadily, _____
11. collaboration, compliance, teamwork, _____

Pattern Words
senior
casual
cordial
brilliant
familiar
behavior
gradually
schedules
persuade
millionaire
procedure
companion

Content Words
spherical
separated
succession
endurance
gymnasium
rectangular
cooperation

A compound subject is made up of two or more subjects that share the same predicate. A compound predicate is made up of two or more predicates that share the same subject.

Write the compound subject and compound predicate in each sentence. The first one is done for you.

12. The coach and the players did persuade the officials and shortened the meeting.
    Compound subject: The coach and the players
    Compound predicate: did persuade the officials and shortened the meeting

Vocabulary Words
capitalism
capitalize
description
subscription

13. The officials and the players separated after the meeting and rested before the match.
    _____
    _____

14. The players and the coach will meet in the gymnasium and discuss their strategy.
    _____
    _____

15. The coach and the team profited from exposure and did capitalize on their status.
    _____
    _____

© Spelling Plus Grade 6   43

A synonym is a word that means the same or almost the same as another word. Read the poem. Write a list word that is a synonym for each underlined word. Use the Spelling Dictionary.

11.4

Writing
Consonants Before i and u

Successful Sportsmanship

A **round** ball was spiked to the ground,
While spectators watched from all around.
The **talented** athlete, with his **well-known** flair,
Smashed the ball through the air.

His **stamina**, **conduct**, and **friendly** play,
Steadily influenced the outcome of the day.
As a **leading** member of his team,
Each **method** was one of esteem.

A detailed **explanation** was not needed for effect,
To **convince** another that his behavior was correct.
When **plans** and goals are going awry,
One may call upon our God most high.

He will remind us to be affectionate to all,
To be of the same mind, and regard His call.
To love and respect an opponent in a game,
Is a behavior of the highest acclaim.

Be kindly affectionate to one another with brotherly love, in honor giving preference to one another.... Be of the same mind toward one another.
Romans 12:10, 16

Pattern Words
senior
casual
cordial
brilliant
familiar
behavior
gradually
schedules
persuade
millionaire
procedure
companion

Content Words
spherical
separated
succession
endurance
gymnasium
rectangular
cooperation

Vocabulary Words
capitalism
capitalize
description
subscription

1. _____
2. _____
3. _____
4. _____
5. _____
6. _____
7. _____
8. _____
9. _____
10. _____
11. _____
12. _____

Name _____

12.1

Review Chapters 7–11
Chapter 7

Pattern Words

Chapter 7 Schwa o	Chapter 8 Schwa in Final Syllables	Chapter 9 Schwa in Unstressed Syllables	Chapter 10 Words with ci, si, ti, and xi	Chapter 11 Consonants Before i and u
collide	trivia	imitate	anxious	senior
eloquent	status	aghast	potential	casual
recollect	bulletin	charity	essential	cordial
collegiate	channel	satellite	explosion	brilliant
concludes	random	algebra	sufficient	familiar
accolades	raucous	apology	beneficial	behavior
configured	versatile	qualified	especially	gradually
committee	broaden	pedestal	distinction	schedules
community	obstinate	diagram	discussion	persuade
unconvinced	intramural	individual	obnoxious	millionaire
recommend	momentous	celebrate	omniscient	procedure
development	accustomed	antiquated	transitional	companion

Content Words

penalties	league	offense	height	spherical
touchdown	athlete	defense	official	separated
scrimmage	statistics	strikers	arenas	succession
interception	amateur	referee	technical	endurance
interference	spectator	association	strategy	gymnasium
quarterback	outfielders	goalkeeper	opponents	rectangular
championship	concessions	tournament	possession	cooperation

Vocabulary Words

dominate	grateful	bilingual	immigrant	capitalism
dominion	gratify	linguistics	migrate	capitalize
opposite	inspire	exposure	disrespectful	description
reposition	inspiring	impose	respectable	subscription

Read Chapter 7 Pattern Words. Follow the directions given.

1. Draw an **X** next to the words with **schwa o** in the first syllable.

2. Circle the words with the **schwa o** in the second syllable.

3. Box the word with the **schwa o** in the third syllable.

Read each word. Decide if it is spelled correctly or incorrectly. Fill in the circle. Write each word correctly.

12.2

Review Chapters 7–11
Chapters 8–9

		Correct	Incorrect	
1.	randem	○	○	_____
2.	channel	○	○	_____
3.	acustomed	○	○	_____
4.	trivea	○	○	_____
5.	intramural	○	○	_____
6.	raucus	○	○	_____
7.	bulletin	○	○	_____
8.	status	○	○	_____
9.	versatal	○	○	_____
10.	obsinat	○	○	_____
11.	broden	○	○	_____
12.	momentous	○	○	_____

trivia
status
bulletin
channel
random
raucous
versatile
broaden
obstinate
intramural
momentous
accustomed

Find the words in the word search. Circle them and write them on the lines. The words go across, down, diagonally, and backwards. Some of the words share letters.

imitate
aghast
charity
satellite
algebra
apology
qualified
pedestal
diagram
individual
celebrate
antiquated

```
a n t i q u a t e d z r a e d e
c p f h k u p s u y l o b t f t
x i o n v y a h t s a h g a c i
w z a l b x t l p e d e s t a l
i d c d o r j m i u q m o i z l
j k d i a g r a m f r i p m l e
c h a r i t y b q s i t a i g t
g w f n v g e t a r b e l e c a
a r b e g l a u d i v i d n i s
```

_____ _____ _____
_____ _____ _____
_____ _____ _____
_____ _____ _____

46

Name _____

12.3

Review Chapters 7–11
Chapters 10–11

	A	B	C	D	E	F	G	H
1	ex	ben	po	suf	sion	ly	sen	ious
2	tial	e	dis	fi	es	ten	plo	cient
3	ob	tinc	anx	nox	tion	cus	pe	cial

anxious
potential
essential
explosion
sufficient
beneficial
especially
distinction
discussion
obnoxious
omniscient
transitional

Find the coordinates given. Use the syllables to write list words.

1. C2 + F3 + E1 = _____
2. A1 + G2 + E1 = _____
3. C3 + H1 = _____
4. B1 + B2 + D2 + H3 = _____
5. C1 + F2 + A2 = _____
6. E2 + G3 + H3 + F1 = _____
7. E2 + G1 + A2 = _____
8. D1 + D2 + H2 = _____
9. A3 + D3 + H1 = _____
10. C2 + B3 + E3 = _____

Write a word that fits each clue. Write each letter in a box.

senior
casual
cordial
brilliant
familiar
behavior
gradually
schedules
persuade
millionaire
procedure
companion

Down
1. informal
2. higher ranking
3. conduct
4. very smart
5. friendly
6. method

Across
7. to convince
8. slowly
9. easily recognized

12.4

Review Chapters 7–11
Content and Vocabulary Words

Read the paragraph. Write a Content Word in each shape box.

Team Sports

Team sports are among the most popular of all sports because they require ▢▢▢▢▢▢▢▢▢▢▢ with teammates to achieve a victory. Professional and ▢▢▢▢▢▢▢ athletes alike enjoy the physicality and ▢▢▢▢▢▢▢▢▢ involved in playing team sports. Whether they play ▢▢▢▢▢▢▢ or ▢▢▢▢▢▢▢, in a ▢▢▢▢▢▢▢▢▢▢ or just for fun, athletes enjoy the competition that team sports provide. If you are an ▢▢▢▢▢▢▢, why not use your God-given abilities and sign up to play team sports?

Word Bank
penalties
interference
championship
athlete
amateur
spectator
offense
defense
tournament
strategy
opponents
possession
endurance
gymnasium
cooperation

Read the meaning of each root. Write the words that contain the given root.

Word Bank
dominate
dominion
reposition
grateful
gratify
inspire
bilingual
linguistics
exposure
immigrant
migrate
disrespectful
capitalism
capitalize
description

1. The root **domin** means **master**.
   _____ _____

2. The root **capit** means **head**.
   _____ _____

3. The root **lingu** means **tongue**.
   _____ _____

4. The root **migr** means **move**.
   _____ _____

5. The root **grat** means **thankful** or **pleasing**.
   _____ _____

6. The root **posit** means **place**.
   _____

48

Name _____

13.2
Word Analysis
Homophones and Homographs

Pattern Words
- council
- counsel
- principal
- principle
- stationary
- stationery
- compliment
- complement
- permit
- content
- contrast
- compact

Homophones are words that sound the same but have different meanings and spellings.

Homographs are words that are spelled alike but have different meanings. They may also be pronounced differently.

Write Pattern Words to complete the exercises.

1.–8. Homophone pairs

9.–12. Homographs according to their pronunciations

1. _____   2. _____
3. _____   4. _____
5. _____   6. _____
7. _____   8. _____

9. /ˈkon trast/ /kən ˈtrast/   10. /ˈpûr mit/ /pûr ˈmit/
   _____   _____

11. /kom ˈpakt/ /kəm ˈpakt/   12. /ˈkon tent/ /kən ˈtent/
    _____   _____

Write Content Words to complete the exercises.

13. Swimmers wear g_____ to protect their eyes from the c_____ in the water.

14. Zachary enjoys participating in swimming, diving, and other a_____.

15. Bethany usually swims the backstroke in the m_____ relay.

16. Caleb's a_____ are amazing when he dives off the s_____.

17. Points range from 0 to 10.5 for the level of d_____ in competitive diving.

Content Words
- medley
- goggles
- chlorine
- aquatics
- difficulty
- acrobatics
- springboard

Vocabulary Words
- dormant
- dormitory
- apparent
- transparency

Challenge Words

_____
_____

swimming

Prefix		Root		Suffix	
ap-	to	dorm	sleep	-ant	state of
trans-	across	it	to go	-ory	place
		par	appear	-ent	inclined
				-ency	quality of

13.2

Vocabulary
Homophones and Homographs

Write the Vocabulary Words.

1. _____   2. _____
3. _____   4. _____

Refer to the table to complete the exercises. Write the word that is being defined.

5. inclined to appear; visible; obvious _____
6. the state of being asleep; inactive _____
7. the quality of light passing through objects so they can be seen from one side to the other side _____
8. a place to go to sleep; a residence hall usually without private bathrooms _____

Write Vocabulary Words to complete the sentences.

9. Joseph and Keith were excited to go to a sports camp and sleep in a _____.
10. It is _____ to Joseph that he could benefit from learning new techniques at camp.
11. The _____ of the water allowed Keith to see the rings he needed to pick up.
12. The flowers that were _____ during the winter finally blossomed and looked pretty near the pool.

Choose the word that matches each definition.

13. a spectacular performance demonstrating agility or complexity
    ○ complement
    ○ springboard
    ○ acrobatics

14. an assortment or mixture
    ○ contrast
    ○ medley
    ○ council

Pattern Words
council
counsel
principal
principle
stationary
stationery
compliment
complement
permit
content
contrast
compact

Content Words
medley
goggles
chlorine
aquatics
difficulty
acrobatics
springboard

Vocabulary Words
dormant
dormitory
apparent
transparency

Name _____

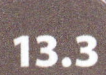

Word Study Strategies
Homophones and Homographs

Refer to the Spelling Dictionary. Write the part of speech and definition of each homograph.

1. /kəm ˈpakt/ _____
2. /kom ˈpakt/ _____
3. /ˈpûr mit/ _____
4. /pûr ˈmit/ _____
5. /kən ˈtrast/ _____
6. /ˈkon trast/ _____
7. /kən ˈtent/ _____
8. /ˈkon tent/ _____

Circle the correct pronunciation for each homograph. Write each homograph.

9. Mom will /kəm ˈpakt/, /kom ˈpakt/ the trash and take it to the curb before the swim meet. _____

10. Coach Thompson does not /ˈpûr mit/, /pûr ˈmit/ the team to dive in the shallow end of the pool. _____

11. The Hemet Hornets' black and gold swimsuits are a striking /kən ˈtrast/, /ˈkon trast/ of colors. _____

12. Adrianna was not /kən ˈtent/, /ˈkon tent/ with her swim time, so she practiced again. _____

Look up each pair of homophones in the Spelling Dictionary. Write the correct homophone to complete each sentence.

principal, principle

13. At the end of the swimming season, the _____ spoke at an award ceremony about one _____ rule of diving.

stationary, stationery

14. Abby used her _____ to thank her grandparents for the new _____ bicycle they gave to her.

complement, compliment

15. Seth paid me a _____ after I installed the springboard to _____ the new pool.

Pattern Words
council
counsel
principal
principle
stationary
stationery
compliment
complement
permit
content
contrast
compact

Content Words
medley
goggles
chlorine
aquatics
difficulty
acrobatics
springboard

Vocabulary Words
dormant
dormitory
apparent
transparency

© Spelling Plus Grade 6   51

Read the letter. Circle the correct homophone or the correct pronunciation of the homograph in the sentences. Correctly write the words below.

13.4

Writing Homophones and Homographs

Dear Hannah,

    I am writing to you on my new <u>stationary, stationery</u> that I received for my birthday. I also received new goggles and a swimsuit, and I cannot wait to use them. My goggles broke a few weeks ago when I was trying to <u>/kəm ˈpakt/, /kom ˈpakt/</u> them along with my towel and flip-flops in my small gym bag. I am excited for swim practice to begin again this year. Although I have not been swimming in several months, I have been quite active. I have been busy building strength by doing calisthenics and riding on the <u>stationary, stationery</u> bicycle. I am hoping that it is apparent to my coach that I am ready to compete in swim meets!

    Last year, I told my coach, who is also the <u>principal, principle</u> of my school, that I wanted to try diving off the springboard and do some acrobatics. He gave me a <u>complement, compliment</u> stating that he knew I would do an awesome job, but he preferred that I remain on the swim team. He said my skills <u>complement, compliment</u> the team since I can do the butterfly stroke well. He went on to say that I would not be able to compete in both swimming and diving events at the meets, and there is not anyone to take my place for the medley relay. My coach's <u>council, counsel</u> made me realize that I should remain on the swim team. The <u>principal, principle</u> rule in diving is to remain streamlined, and I happen to have difficulty with that skill when diving. I know I would get better with practice, but I am <u>/ˈkon tent/, /kən ˈtent/</u> to stay on the swim team. There is a lot of God-given talent on our swim team, and we all enjoy each other's company.

    Perhaps you can visit sometime this month, attend a swim meet, and meet my teammates. I would really enjoy having you as my guest. If your parents <u>/pûr ˈmit/, /ˈpûr mit/</u> you to come, I know my parents would enjoy having you. After all, we are cousins! I will ask Mom to call Aunt Janell to arrange a weekend that you can stay with us. It will be fun!

                                             Sincerely,
                                               Kadeishah

Pattern Words

council
counsel
principal
principle
stationary
stationery
compliment
complement
permit
content
contrast
compact

Content Words

medley
goggles
chlorine
aquatics
difficulty
acrobatics
springboard

Vocabulary Words

dormant
dormitory
apparent
transparency

1. _____   2. _____   3. _____
4. _____   5. _____   6. _____
7. _____   8. _____   9. _____
10. _____

Name _____

14.2 Word Analysis — Compound Words

Pattern Words
- waterline
- backache
- widespread
- praiseworthy
- beachcombing
- locker room
- swimming pool
- common sense
- community center
- left-handed
- able-bodied
- well-conditioned

Content Words
- interval
- buoyant
- handling
- versions
- infraction
- substitute
- identification

Vocabulary Words
- finally
- refine
- dissolve
- resolved

A compound word is made of two or more smaller words. Compound words can be closed, open, or hyphenated.

Write Pattern Words to complete the exercises. Sort the compound words.

1.–3. Hyphenated compound words   4.–8. Closed compound words
9.–12. Open compound words

1. _____   2. _____
3. _____   4. _____
5. _____   6. _____
7. _____   8. _____
9. _____   10. _____
11. _____   12. _____

Write Content Words to complete the exercises.

13. In the sport of water polo, a b_____ ball is thrown into a netted goal.

14. There are different v_____ of water polo.

15. A water-polo team is comprised of a goalkeeper and six players, and can have up to six s_____ players. Players wear caps of different colors for i_____.

16. A water-polo match is divided into four time periods with a resting i_____ between each period.

17. With the exception of the goalkeeper, water-polo players may not use two hands when h_____ the ball. An i_____ of this rule and others can result in penalties.

Challenge Words
_____
_____

water polo

Prefix		Root		Suffix	
re-	again	fin	end	-al	related to
dis-	apart	solv	loosen, solve	-ly	forms an adverb from an adjective
				-ed	makes verbs past tense

14.2

Vocabulary
Compound Words

Pattern Words

waterline
backache
widespread
praiseworthy
beachcombing
locker room
swimming pool
common sense
community center
left-handed
able-bodied
well-conditioned

Content Words

interval
buoyant
handling
versions
infraction
substitute
identification

Vocabulary Words

finally
refine
dissolve
resolved

Write the Vocabulary Words.

1. _____
2. _____
3. _____
4. _____

Refer to the table to complete the exercises. Match each word to its definition.

_____ 5. dissolve   a. to improve or perfect again
_____ 6. refine   b. related to the end of a series or process; at last
_____ 7. resolved   c. to loosen or melt apart
_____ 8. finally   d. to have determined, solved, or settled

Write Vocabulary Words to complete the sentences.

9. The maintenance technician pours chemicals into the pool so they can _____ before water-polo practice.

10. The team _____ to train hard so that they could do well in the national meet for water polo.

11. To prepare for the national meet, the coach wanted the team to _____ their swimming, treading, passing, and throwing techniques.

12. _____, after three weeks, practice came to an end, and the team felt confident and prepared for the national meet.

13. The coaching staff and the entire team _____ to do their best to _____ as many technical aspects of water polo as possible before the important championship match.

54

Name _____

14.3

Word Study Strategies
Compound Words

Use the Spelling Dictionary to answer each question.
1. What is the pronunciation for **waterline**? _____
2. What is the part of speech for **well-conditioned**? _____
3. What is the definition for **common sense**? _____
4. What is the sample sentence for **finally**? _____
   _____
5. What is the pronunciation for **praiseworthy**? _____
6. What is the part of speech for **left-handed**? _____
7. What is the sample sentence for **locker room**? _____
   _____
8. What are the definitions for **buoyant**? _____
   _____
9. What are the sample sentences for **buoyant**? _____
   _____
   _____

Pattern Words
waterline
backache
widespread
praiseworthy
beachcombing
locker room
swimming pool
common sense
community center
left-handed
able-bodied
well-conditioned

Content Words
interval
buoyant
handling
versions
infraction
substitute
identification

Vocabulary Words
finally
refine
dissolve
resolved

A <mark>conjunction</mark> is a word that is used to join words or groups of words. A <mark>coordinating conjunction</mark> is a word that is used to join words that have the same function. Some coordinating conjunctions are *and*, *so*, *or*, and *but*.

Read each sentence and underline the conjunction. Locate the list words in each sentence and write them. The first one is done for you.
10. Luke <u>and</u> Taryn are well-conditioned athletes. _____well-conditioned_____
11. Myrna is a left-handed athlete, so she is a unique asset to the team.
    _____
12. The large swimming pool is heated, and the community center is open year-round. _____ _____
13. Have you seen or heard the widespread report on the water-polo team's praiseworthy efforts? _____ _____
14. The team could not refine their throwing skills during drills, but they resolved to practice diligently. _____ _____

Finally, brethren, whatever things are true, whatever things are noble, whatever things are just, whatever things are pure, whatever things are lovely, whatever things are of good report, if there is any virtue and if there is anything praiseworthy—meditate on these things. Philippians 4:8

Jem and Krysta designed a scrapbook page about water polo. Read the captions on the scrapbook page. Choose a list word to complete each sentence. Write each word below.

14.4

Writing Compound Words

Jem, being an __1__ athlete, was crucial to our team's victory at the playoffs! She trains for two hours every morning. Jem enjoys her time in the cool water of the __2__.

One of Jem's strengths is that she does not use her right hand. Jem is __3__ which makes her a strong, right-wing defender. Her throwing technique of the __4__ ball is exemplary and __5__.

Krysta __6__ to use Jem's example to motivate her to __7__ her skills in water polo. Since Jem and Krysta are best friends, Jem helped Krysta become a __8__ athlete before the playoffs.

With Jem's guidance, Krysta improved and perfected the technique of __9__ the water-polo ball. Because of all the preparation and practice, it was a great water-polo season!

Pattern Words
waterline
backache
widespread
praiseworthy
beachcombing
locker room
swimming pool
common sense
community center
left-handed
able-bodied
well-conditioned

Content Words
interval
buoyant
handling
versions
infraction
substitute
identification

Vocabulary Words
finally
refine
dissolve
resolved

1. _____
2. _____
3. _____
4. _____
5. _____
6. _____
7. _____
8. _____
9. _____

56

Name _____

15.2 Word Analysis Endings

Pattern Words
- since
- sense
- intense
- diligence
- convince
- pretense
- condense
- assistance
- resistance
- excellence
- experience
- independence

Write Pattern Words to complete the exercises.
Sort the words according to their ending.

1.–8. **nce**   9.–12. **nse**

1. _____   2. _____
3. _____   4. _____
5. _____   6. _____
7. _____   8. _____
9. _____   10. _____
11. _____   12. _____

Write Content Words to complete the exercises.

13. Waterskiing is a sport enjoyed for both recreation and c_____.

14. Water-skiers grip a t_____ that is attached to a motorboat as it a_____.

15. H_____ is skimming the surface of the water.

16. Whether they are using skis or b_____ on bare feet, water-skiers remain p_____ to the surface of the water.

17. Competitive water-skiers can execute tricks and a_____ maneuvers above the surface of the water.

Content Words
- aerial
- towrope
- balancing
- competition
- accelerates
- hydroplaning
- perpendicular

For you were bought at a price; therefore glorify God in your body and in your spirit, which are God's.
1 Corinthians 6:20

Vocabulary Words
- inflection
- reflected
- functional
- malfunction

Challenge Words
_____
_____

waterskiing

15.2 Vocabulary Endings

Prefix		Root		Suffix	
in-	in	flect	bend	-ion	state of
re-	back	funct	perform	-ed	makes verbs past tense
mal-	bad			-al	related to

Pattern Words
since
sense
intense
diligence
convince
pretense
condense
assistance
resistance
excellence
experience
independence

Content Words
aerial
towrope
balancing
competition
accelerates
hydroplaning
perpendicular

Vocabulary Words
inflection
reflected
functional
malfunction

Write the Vocabulary Words.

1. _____
2. _____
3. _____
4. _____

Refer to the table to complete the exercises. Write the word that is being defined.

5. light bent back into one's eyes _____
6. the state of performing _____
7. the state of having a change in the pitch of one's voice _____
8. a state of performing badly; a breakdown _____

Write Vocabulary Words to complete the sentences.

9. It was a hot summer day, and the sunlight _____ off the water of the Chesapeake Bay.
10. The water-skiers decided to rent a _____ motorboat.
11. By the _____ in their voices, it was clear that they were ecstatic about having a day to ski.
12. As soon as the group left the dock, the motorboat began to _____. Taking the boat in for repairs would postpone their escapade for a while.

Choose the word that matches each definition.

13. perseverance in performing one's obligations
    ○ diligence   ○ convince   ○ excellence
14. to make more compact
    ○ independence   ○ condense   ○ since
15. to an extreme degree
    ○ assistance   ○ sense   ○ intense

58

Name _____

15.3
Word Study Strategies
Endings

Write a list word that is a related form of each group of words.

1. dependable, dependent, interdependent, _____
2. expert, expertise, experiential, _____
3. decelerate, accelerate, accelerated, _____

Related word forms can be different parts of speech. Change each verb to make it a noun. Write the list word.

4. excel _____
5. assist _____
6. resist _____
7. inflect _____
8. pretend _____
9. compete _____

Some words have more than one definition. Words with more than one definition can also have more than one part of speech.

Write a list word to complete each sentence. Then use the Spelling Dictionary to write the part of speech and the number of the definition that matches the way the word is used in the sentence.

10. My parents taught me to water-ski, and I have loved to ski ever _____.

    Part of speech: _____   Definition number: _____

11. My _____ of balance on water skis keeps me steady.

    Part of speech: _____   Definition number: _____

12. It takes _____ concentration to perform many of the tricks that professionals are able to perform on water skis.

    Part of speech: _____   Definition number: _____

13. _____ I learned a new technique for waterskiing, I decided to try it out.

    Part of speech: _____   Definition number: _____

14. I _____ that my new technique will improve my skiing.

    Part of speech: _____   Definition number: _____

15. I hope that the wind will not be too _____ for waterskiing tomorrow.

    Part of speech: _____   Definition number: _____

Pattern Words
since
sense
intense
diligence
convince
pretense
condense
assistance
resistance
excellence
experience
independence

Content Words
aerial
towrope
balancing
competition
accelerates
hydroplaning
perpendicular

Vocabulary Words
inflection
reflected
functional
malfunction

A run-on sentence is an incorrect combination of two or more complete sentences. Revise and perfect the narrative and solutions about waterskiing. Use proofreading marks. Correctly write the misspelled words.

15.4
Writing Endings

Summer Fun

Last summer my friends and I longed for independance and fun, so we decided to convince our parents that we were old enough to go waterskiing on our nearby lake My friends Christy, Mack, and I arrived at the dock where we were able to rent a motorboat. christy and I put our skis in the back of the boat. We used diligense in checking all the vital parts of the boat to be certain that it was functionel. The towrope was sturdy and the engine looked good. This was going to be an experiense that we would all all remember!

    Soon we were out in middle of the Lake. The intense sun refleckted off the water, but we were cooled by the spray fanning out behind our skis. We skimmed over the water. Hydroplanning across the surface of the lake was so much fun! However, I could sence that something was wrong the engine began to make a strange noise, signaling a malfunction. Soon, it quit altogether. The three of us us had a real problem; we were stranded in the middle of a lake!

We had two possible solutions.

Solution 1: Since there were other boats on the lake, we could have yelled for assistence from another boater, but we might not have been heard

Solution 2: We could have used our skis as paddles and tried to reach the shore by rowing, but the resistanse of the water would have made rowing very tiring.

Proofreading Marks
- ◯ Circle misspellings.
- ≡ Make a capital letter.
- ⊙ Add a period.
- ⸕ Delete.
- ∧ Add something.
- / Make a small letter.
- ¶ Make a new paragraph.

Pattern Words
since
sense
intense
diligence
convince
pretense
condense
assistance
resistance
excellence
experience
independence

Content Words
aerial
towrope
balancing
competition
accelerates
hydroplaning
perpendicular

Vocabulary Words
inflection
reflected
functional
malfunction

1. _____ 2. _____ 3. _____
4. _____ 5. _____ 6. _____
7. _____ 8. _____ 9. _____

Locate the run-on sentence in the narrative and rewrite it as two complete sentences.

10. _____

11. _____

12. On a separate piece of paper, complete the narrative by choosing either of the solutions or by writing one of your own. Use at least three list words and proofread your work.

Name _____

16.2
Word Analysis
Endings

Pattern Words
- resilient
- relevant
- pleasant
- gradient
- constant
- adjacent
- frequent
- reluctant
- applicant
- confident
- significant
- absorbent

Write Pattern Words to complete the exercises.
Sort the words according to their ending.

1.–6. **ant**   7.–12. **ent**

1. _____   2. _____
3. _____   4. _____
5. _____   6. _____
7. _____   8. _____
9. _____   10. _____
11. _____   12. _____

Write Content Words to complete the exercises.

13. Scull racing, also called s_____, involves one to four rowers who each use a pair of oars and face the stern.

14. The r_____ of a rower's s_____ is essential in rowing.

15. The consistently repetitive strokes p_____ a boat through the water.

16. A canoeist or kayaker must learn to quickly n_____ turns when navigating through fast-moving, dangerous waters.

17. The c_____ of kayaks, canoes, and rowboats differs from each other.

18. Rowboats are built on a wooden or fiber f_____, whereas canoes and kayaks are constructed of molded plastic, aluminum, and other materials.

Content Words
- propel
- sculling
- rhythm
- strokes
- negotiate
- framework
- construction

Vocabulary Words
- confined
- confinement
- sedentary
- supersede

Challenge Words

_____

_____

rowing

16.2 Vocabulary Endings

Prefix		Root		Suffix	
con-	thoroughly	fin	end	-ed	makes verbs past tense
super-	higher	sed	sit	-ment	that which
				-ent	inclined to
				-ary	of

Pattern Words
resilient
relevant
pleasant
gradient
constant
adjacent
frequent
reluctant
applicant
confident
significant
absorbent

Content Words
propel
sculling
rhythm
strokes
negotiate
framework
construction

Vocabulary Words
confined
confinement
sedentary
supersede

Write the Vocabulary Words.

1. _____
2. _____
3. _____
4. _____

Refer to the table to complete the exercises. Match each word to its definition.

_____ 5. confined   a. inclined to sit; inactive

_____ 6. confinement   b. to have thoroughly kept within a boundary

_____ 7. sedentary   c. that which is being thoroughly kept within a boundary

_____ 8. supersede   d. to replace with higher qualities

Write Vocabulary Words to complete the sentences.

9. The _____ of water by a dam forms a lake upon which water sports may be enjoyed.

10. In a river, water is _____ between two banks.

11. Although sitting is involved in canoeing, it is not a _____ sport because it involves actively propelling the canoe.

12. The advancement of technology allows new and improved design and construction of boats, canoes, and kayaks to _____ older, antiquated models.

Choose the best meaning for each underlined word.

13. Wearing a life vest is <u>important</u> to survival if one is ejected from a kayak.
    ○ applicant   ○ significant   ○ absorbent

14. A person should be <u>unwilling</u> to go kayaking if a life vest is unavailable.
    ○ reluctant   ○ gradient   ○ adjacent

Name _____

An antonym is a word that means the opposite of another word. Write a list word that is an antonym for each word.

	harsh		free
1.	_____	2.	_____
	active		uncertain
3.	_____	4.	_____
	distant		repellent
5.	_____	6.	_____
	seldom		unimportant
7.	_____	8.	_____
	inconsistent		eager
9.	_____	10.	_____

Word Study Strategies
Endings

Pattern Words
resilient
relevant
pleasant
gradient
constant
adjacent
frequent
reluctant
applicant
confident
significant
absorbent

Content Words
propel
sculling
rhythm
strokes
negotiate
framework
construction

Vocabulary Words
confined
confinement
sedentary
supersede

A simple sentence expresses a complete thought. A compound sentence is made up of two or more simple sentences that are linked with a comma and a coordinating conjunction. Some coordinating conjunctions are *and*, *so*, *or*, and *but*.

Combine each set of simple sentences into a compound sentence. Use a comma and a coordinating conjunction.

11. Max is confident that he can negotiate the kayak through the rapids. Cara is reluctant to go with him.

   _____
   _____

12. The weather is warm and pleasant. Xavier is going sculling.

   _____
   _____

13. Paddles are used to propel a canoe. The constant rhythm of strokes is significant.

   _____
   _____

14. Walker and Aubrey will go rowing on Saturday. They will be confined to the house if it is raining.

   _____
   _____

Read the narrative about the boat race. Write the list words that could replace the bold words in each sentence. Use the Spelling Dictionary for reference.

16.4
Writing Endings

The Boat Race

Today Magnus and I were a pair in competitive **scull racing**. We arrived at Lake Hodges at 6:00 A.M. in order to check in, receive our entry number, and launch the boat from the dock before the race began. Excitement filled the air as each **candidate**, now contestant, for the race began to arrive. To ease our minds, Magnus and I conversed about his new truck, our jobs, and other things not **pertaining** to the boat race. Before we knew it, it was time for the race to begin. We put on our life vests and boarded the boat.

As the race began, Magnus and I pulled on our oars to **drive** our boat through the water. The **consistent** **repetition** of our **unbroken movements** quickly put us in the lead. I was a bit nervous because I did not want to be in the lead so early in the race. Strategy is **important** in any competition, and Magnus and I do not like to take the lead until we are nearing the end of the race. This allows us to preserve our energy and sprint to the finish line. Soon, another pair moved ahead of us. However, I was not worried and was **certain** that we would regain the lead. After all, Magnus and I had been in several competitions together and won races even though we had lagged behind earlier in the race. This race was no different. Two more boats pulled ahead of us. I still felt confident. I could feel the energy begin to surge inside my body as we began to **travel successfully along** to the finish line. Instantaneously, Magnus and I began to increase our speed. We were sprinting toward the finish line! I could hear the crowds cheering on the platform that was **adjoining** the dock. We finally crossed the finish line and were quickly informed that we had won the race!

Pattern Words
resilient
relevant
pleasant
gradient
constant
adjacent
frequent
reluctant
applicant
confident
significant
absorbent

Content Words
propel
sculling
rhythm
strokes
negotiate
framework
construction

Vocabulary Words
confined
confinement
sedentary
supersede

1. _____ 2. _____ 3. _____
4. _____ 5. _____ 6. _____
7. _____ 8. _____ 9. _____
10. _____ 11. _____

12. On a separate piece of paper, write a different ending to the narrative. Use list words.

Name _____

17.2 Word Analysis — Endings

Pattern Words

illusion
crucial
ambition
impartial
occasion
exception
superficial
substantial
profession
trepidation
intermission
exclamation

Content Words

agility
paddling
equilibrium
dimensions
challenging
surfboards
momentum

Vocabulary Words

refinish
unfinished
flexible
inflexible

Write Pattern Words to complete the exercises.
Sort the words according to their ending.

1.–2. **cial**   3.–6. **sion**   7.–8. **tial**   9.–12. **tion**

1. _____   2. _____
3. _____   4. _____
5. _____   6. _____
7. _____   8. _____
9. _____   10. _____
11. _____ 12. _____

Write Content Words to complete the exercises.

13. Surfing is a c_____ sport that requires a great deal of a_____.

14. After p_____ out to the line of breaking surf, a surfer has to maintain his or her e_____ while standing upright on the surfboard.

15. Surfers use the m_____ of the breaking wave to ride across the wave's surface and on the crest of the wave.

16. There are several different types of s_____ and their d_____ vary.

> The Lord is my strength and song,
> And He has become my salvation;
> He is my God, and I will praise Him;
> My father's God, and I will exalt Him
> Exodus 15:2

Challenge Words

_____
_____

surfing

17.2 Vocabulary Endings

Prefix		Root		Suffix	
re-	again	fin	end	-ish	process of
un-	not	flex	bend	-ed	makes verb past tense
in-	not			-ible	is able

Pattern Words
illusion
crucial
ambition
impartial
occasion
exception
superficial
substantial
profession
trepidation
intermission
exclamation

Content Words
agility
paddling
equilibrium
dimensions
challenging
surfboards
momentum

Vocabulary Words
refinish
unfinished
flexible
inflexible

Write the Vocabulary Words.

1. _____
2. _____
3. _____
4. _____

Refer to the table to complete the exercises. Write the word that is being defined.

5. not yet at an end; incomplete _____
6. not able to be bent; unbendable _____
7. the process of finishing again; redo _____
8. able to be bent; adaptable _____

Write Vocabulary Words to complete the sentences.

9. I have always preferred body surfing, so my brother Daron encouraged me to be _____ and try surfing on a surfboard.
10. Daron had his own board, but we had to _____ one of our dad's old boards for me to use.
11. The board was made of a foam core with added fiberglass and resin to make it stiff and _____.
12. Daron gave me a few surfing lessons before we went out on the water, but my surfing education is still _____.

Choose the best meaning for each underlined word.

13. Rachael approached learning to surf with <u>trepidation</u>.
    ○ fear   ○ delay   ○ balance
14. Her <u>ambition</u> is to become an excellent surfer.
    ○ honesty   ○ desire to achieve   ○ role
15. Rachael's surfboard has decals and other <u>superficial</u> designs.
    ○ ordinary   ○ engraved   ○ on the surface
16. She enjoys surfing but would not choose it as a <u>profession</u>.
    ○ career   ○ hobby   ○ substitute

Name _____

17.3
Word Study Strategies
Endings

An analogy is made up of two word pairs. Both pairs of words have the same kind of relationship. Complete each analogy with a list word.

1. **Sunlight** is to **moonlight** as **clumsiness** is to _____.
2. **Achieve** is to **succeed** as **difficult** is to _____.
3. **Unsteady** is to **shaky** as **incomplete** is to _____.
4. **Pleasant** is to **disagreeable** as **confidence** is to _____.
5. **Movable** is to **immovable** as **flexible** is to _____.
6. **Total** is to **complete** as **essential** is to _____.
7. **Sunset** is to **sunrise** as **hobby** is to _____.
8. **Reluctant** is to **eager** as **deep** is to _____.
9. **Revise** is to **redo** as **repair** is to _____.

A simple sentence expresses a complete thought. A compound sentence is made up of two or more simple sentences that are linked with a comma and a coordinating conjunction. Some coordinating conjunctions are *and*, *so*, *or*, and *but*.

Combine each set of simple sentences into a compound sentence. Use commas and coordinating conjunctions. The same conjunction can be used twice.

10. Lia loves to surf. Her ambition is to become a professional surfer. She practices every day.

_____

_____

11. The dimensions of surfboards vary in length. They also vary in width. They all weigh less than fifteen pounds.

_____

_____

12. Nate refinishes surfboards. He may refinish one of his older boards today. He may leave it unfinished until tomorrow.

_____

_____

_____

Pattern Words
illusion
crucial
ambition
impartial
occasion
exception
superficial
substantial
profession
trepidation
intermission
exclamation

Content Words
agility
paddling
equilibrium
dimensions
challenging
surfboards
momentum

Vocabulary Words
refinish
unfinished
flexible
inflexible

A synonym is a word that means the same or almost the same as another word. Read the narrative. Write a list word that is a synonym for each underlined word. Use the Spelling Dictionary.

17.4
Writing Endings

Surfing at Waimea Bay

My older brother Reid has a unique **career**. He is a surfer. Not everyone is able to make a living by surfing, but my brother does. He enters surfing competitions that offer prize money. Reid also receives **ample** income from advertising surfboards.

I watched a recent surfing competition at Waimea Bay, Hawaii. Reid was one of the contestants. It was a bright, beautiful day with very high surf. The waves were huge! I asked Reid if he ever felt **fear** when the waves were that big. He told me that it was **essential** to focus primarily on the break of the wave and to assess its **measurements**. Soon, it was Reid's turn to surf. He began paddling toward the line of breaking waves. He used his agility to get to his feet immediately. The momentum of the wave propelled him across the face of the wave, just under its crest. Reid maintained his **balance** on the board and rode the wave. He had a long ride on a **difficult** wave. The next wave broke much faster, so Reid could not ride as long, but he did show the judges how **adaptable** he was to various surf conditions. It was all Reid could do to hang on to his board on the final, monstrous wave. I prayed for Reid as he disappeared into the tube of the wave, reappearing on the other side.

Reid scored very well because the surfing judges were **fair**. Although Reid did not win this competition, he did take second place. I realized that I was very proud of the job that he did. I am thinking about becoming a professional surfer, too.

Pattern Words
illusion
crucial
ambition
impartial
occasion
exception
superficial
substantial
profession
trepidation
intermission
exclamation

Content Words
agility
paddling
equilibrium
dimensions
challenging
surfboards
momentum

Vocabulary Words
refinish
unfinished
flexible
inflexible

1. _____ 2. _____ 3. _____
4. _____ 5. _____ 6. _____
7. _____ 8. _____ 9. _____

10. On a separate piece of paper, write about a sport experience that you have had. Use a graphic organizer to plan your narrative. Use several list words. Proofread your work.

Name _____

18.1

Review Chapters 13–17
Chapter 13

Pattern Words

Chapter 13	Chapter 14	Chapter 15	Chapter 16	Chapter 17
Homophones and Homographs	Compound Words	Endings	Endings	Endings
council	waterline	since	resilient	illusion
counsel	backache	sense	relevant	crucial
principal	widespread	intense	pleasant	ambition
principle	praiseworthy	diligence	gradient	impartial
stationary	beachcombing	convince	constant	occasion
stationery	locker room	pretense	adjacent	exception
compliment	swimming pool	condense	frequent	superficial
complement	common sense	assistance	reluctant	substantial
permit	community center	resistance	applicant	profession
content	left-handed	excellence	confident	trepidation
contrast	able-bodied	experience	significant	intermission
compact	well-conditioned	independence	absorbent	exclamation

Content Words

medley	interval	aerial	propel	agility
goggles	buoyant	towrope	sculling	paddling
chlorine	handling	balancing	rhythm	equilibrium
aquatics	versions	competition	strokes	dimensions
difficulty	infraction	accelerates	negotiate	challenging
acrobatics	substitute	hydroplaning	framework	surfboards
springboard	identification	perpendicular	construction	momentum

Vocabulary Words

dormant	finally	inflection	confined	refinish
dormitory	refine	reflected	confinement	unfinished
apparent	dissolve	functional	sedentary	flexible
transparency	resolved	malfunction	supersede	inflexible

Read Chapter 13 Pattern Words. Follow the directions given.
1. Circle the homophone pairs. 2. Underline the homographs.
Read the pronunciations and write the homograph.
3. /'kon trast/ /kən 'trast/   4. /pûr 'mit/ /'pûr mit/
   _____   _____

Complete the sentence with homophones.
5. Mr. Lo, the _____, paid me a _____ when he wrote a note on _____, providing me his _____.

18.2

Combine a word from each column to form a closed, open, or hyphenated compound word from the list. Write each word.

Review Chapters 13–17
Chapters 14–15

able	handed
locker	bodied
beach	line
common	spread
wide	room
back	sense
left	pool
praise	center
well	worthy
swimming	combing
water	ache
community	conditioned

Word list:
- waterline
- backache
- widespread
- praiseworthy
- beachcombing
- locker room
- swimming pool
- common sense
- community center
- left-handed
- able-bodied
- well-conditioned

1. _____
2. _____
3. _____
4. _____
5. _____
6. _____
7. _____
8. _____
9. _____
10. _____
11. _____
12. _____

Read each word. Decide if it is spelled correctly or incorrectly. Fill in the circle. Write each word correctly.

Word bank:
- since
- sense
- intense
- diligence
- convince
- pretense
- condense
- assistance
- resistance
- excellence
- experience
- independence

#	Word	Correct	Incorrect
13.	since	○	○
14.	inntence	○	○
15.	resistense	○	○
16.	pretense	○	○
17.	expiriense	○	○
18.	sense	○	○
19.	excellence	○	○
20.	kondence	○	○
21.	diligence	○	○
22.	indipendance	○	○
23.	convince	○	○
24.	asistense	○	○

Name _____

18.3

Review Chapters 13–17
Chapters 16–17

Write the missing letters to complete the acrostic. The circled letter is a hint for the ending spelling.

1. __ o n __ i __ ⃝ n __
2. **a** b __ __ r __ ⃝ __ t
3. __ **r** e __ u __ ⃝ n __
4. c __ n **s** __ ⃝ n __

and

5. __ p **p** __ __ c __ ⃝ n __
6. p __ __ **a** __ ⃝ __ t
7. __ **d** j a __ ⃝ n __
8. **g** __ a **d** __ ⃝ __ __
9. r __ **l** __ v __ __ t
10. __ **e** l __ __ __ ⃝ n t
11. r __ **s** __ l __ ⃝ n t

resilient
relevant
pleasant
gradient
constant
adjacent
frequent
reluctant
applicant
confident
significant
absorbent

Rearrange the syllables and cross out the unnecessary syllable to form a list word. Write each word.

illusion
crucial
ambition
impartial
occasion
exception
superficial
substantial
profession
trepidation
intermission
exclamation

sion ca tial oc
12. _____

su fi tion per cial
14. _____

tion da i cial trep
16. _____

ter sion in mis tial
18. _____

sion ex tion cep
20. _____

tial im sion par
13. _____

tial pro sion fes
15. _____

tion cial am bi
17. _____

ex ma tion cla cial
19. _____

cial tial stan sub
21. _____

18.4

Review Chapters 13–17
Content and Vocabulary Words

Write the Content Word that answers each riddle.

1. Which word is a contest? _____
2. Which word implies balance? _____
3. Which word is being built? _____
4. Which word is a chemical? _____
5. Which word skims the water? _____
6. Which word occurs in the air? _____
7. Which word is a replacement? _____
8. Which word is a failure to obey? _____
9. Which word protects your eyes? _____
10. Which word proves who you are? _____
11. Which word is a skeletal structure? _____
12. Which word is not easy to achieve? _____
13. Which word is able to move quickly? _____
14. Which word provides measurements? _____
15. Which word moves you forward by force? _____

goggles
chlorine
difficulty
infraction
substitute
identification
aerial
competition
hydroplaning
propel
framework
construction
agility
equilibrium
dimensions

Read the meaning of each root. Write the Vocabulary Words that contain the given root.

dormant
dormitory
apparent
finally
dissolve
resolved
inflection
reflected
functional
confined
sedentary
supersede
refinish
flexible
inflexible

16. The root **solv** means **loosen** or **solve**.
    _____ _____

17. The root **dorm** means **sleep**.
    _____ _____

18. The root **sed** means **sit**.
    _____ _____

19. The root **flect** or **flex** means **bend**.
    _____ _____
    _____ _____

20. The root **fin** means **end**.
    _____ _____
    _____

21. The root **par** means **appear**.
    _____

Name _____

19.2 Word Analysis — Greek Roots

Pattern Words

cardiology
cardiopathy
cardiogram
cardiograph
hydropathy
hydroscope
hydrotherapy
hydrothermal
thermostat
thermogenic
thermometer
thermography

Content Words

deuce
velocity
aerobic
diagonally
advantage
boundaries
professionals

Vocabulary Words

arbitrate
arbitrary
perspiration
respiration

Greek roots are used to build many words in the English language. A root is the part of a word that gives the basic meaning. Knowledge of word origins helps in building spelling and vocabulary skills.

Write Pattern Words to complete the exercises. Sort by Greek roots.

1.–4. **hydro**   5.–8. **cardio**   9.–12. **thermo**

1. _____   2. _____
3. _____   4. _____
5. _____   6. _____
7. _____   8. _____
9. _____   10. _____
11. _____ 12. _____

Write Content Words to complete the exercises.

13. A tennis court has sideline b_____ for singles and doubles play.
14. The server must hit the ball so that it lands in the service box, d_____ opposite of the server.
15. The v_____ of a tennis serve by some p_____ has reached over one hundred miles per hour.
16. When the score is d_____, the player who wins the next point has the a_____.
17. Tennis is an a_____ sport because it is an action-filled game that increases your heart rate.

Challenge Words

_____
_____

tennis

19.2 Vocabulary — Greek Roots

Prefix		Root		Suffix	
per-	through	arbitr	judge	-ate	to act
re-	again	spir	breathe	-ary	related to
				-ation	state of

Pattern Words
cardiology
cardiopathy
cardiogram
cardiograph
hydropathy
hydroscope
hydrotherapy
hydrothermal
thermostat
thermogenic
thermometer
thermography

Content Words
deuce
velocity
aerobic
diagonally
advantage
boundaries
professionals

Vocabulary Words
arbitrate
arbitrary
perspiration
respiration

Write the Vocabulary Words.

1. _____
2. _____
3. _____
4. _____

Refer to the table to complete the exercises. Write the word that is being defined.

5. related to a personal decision or judgment; random _____
6. the state of secreting sweat through the skin; sweat _____
7. to act as a judge to make a decision _____
8. the state of breathing _____

Write Vocabulary Words to complete the sentences.

9. Claire will _____ Annie and Ida's tennis match to ensure the line calls are fair.
10. Claire is known for making fair, not _____, decisions.
11. Ida could hear Annie's heavy _____ during the exciting, close match.
12. During Ida and Annie's tennis match, their exertion resulted in _____.

Choose the best meaning for each word.

13. velocity
    ○ speed
    ○ volume
    ○ length

14. hydrothermal
    ○ relating to cold water
    ○ relating to salt water
    ○ relating to hot water

15. boundaries
    ○ results
    ○ limits
    ○ objects

16. cardiopathy
    ○ a disease or disorder of the heart
    ○ a disease or disorder of the eye
    ○ a disease or disorder of the liver

Name _____

19.3

Word Study Strategies
Greek Roots

Greek Roots

cardio = heart	gen = produce	gram = write	graph = write
hydro = water	logy = study of	meter = measure	path = disease
scop = see	stat = stand	therap = treatment	therm = heat
thermo = heat			

Pattern Words
cardiology
cardiopathy
cardiogram
cardiograph
hydropathy
hydroscope
hydrotherapy
hydrothermal
thermostat
thermogenic
thermometer
thermography

Refer to the Greek roots. Circle the common Greek root in each set of words. Write the root to complete the sentences.

1. thermostat, thermogenic, thermometer, thermography

   The Greek root _____ means *heat*.

2. cardiology, cardiopathy, cardiogram, cardiograph

   The Greek root _____ means *heart*.

3. hydropathy, hydroscope, hydrotherapy, hydrothermal

   The Greek root _____ means *water*.

Use the information about Greek roots to complete each exercise. Write the Pattern Words that reflect the combined Greek root meanings.

heat + produce   heart + write

4. _____   5. _____

water + heat   heart + study of

6. _____   7. _____

water + see   heat + measure

8. _____   9. _____

Content Words
deuce
velocity
aerobic
diagonally
advantage
boundaries
professionals

A sentence fragment is an incomplete sentence that does not express a complete thought. A fragment is missing the subject, predicate, or both. Write a complete sentence from each fragment. The first one is done for you.

10. The boundaries on a tennis court. The white lines show the boundaries on a tennis court.

11. The thermostat in the gym. _____

12. During the summer, many professionals. _____

Vocabulary Words
arbitrate
arbitrary
perspiration
respiration

Read Dr. Spiering's persuasive essay about tennis. Write the correct list word for each bold word or words below. Use the Spelling Dictionary.

19.4
Writing Greek Roots

The Benefits of Tennis

As a doctor, I am involved in **the study of the heart and treatment of disorders and diseases** and examine patients with **a disease or disorder of the heart**. It is no secret that heart disease is avoidable with proper diet and exercise. Proper exercise raises one's heart rate and affects his or her **state of breathing**. An intense aerobic activity will produce **sweat** and should be a part of everyone's weekly routine—not just **people receiving a financial gain for their skills in sports**. Exercise can be as simple as taking a walk around the neighborhood or as challenging as training for a marathon.

The sport I highly recommend is tennis. Do you know there is more than one **benefit** to playing tennis? It has been called the "sport of a lifetime" because it offers health, psychological, and social benefits. Health benefits include strengthening muscles by serving or returning balls to opponents with a high **speed**, improving agility by hitting balls before they go outside the **limits**, burning calories, and reducing the risk of cardiovascular events such as heart attack or stroke. Psychological benefits include keeping the brain mentally sharp by thinking constantly about where to hit the ball, being able to make fair decisions that are not **random**, and reducing anxiety and tension while increasing optimism, vigor, and self-esteem. Social benefits include opportunities to join tennis clubs, frequent public courts, interact with opponents in singles, doubles, and mixed leagues of competition, and build relationships within the family by making it a family sport. Since tennis is enjoyed by people young and old, the sport provides opportunities to build intergenerational relationships.

Whether you play tennis or not, I strongly urge you to participate in an invigorating, enjoyable sport that is **increasing oxygen consumption in the body**. God created us in a wonderful way, and we need to take care of the body He has given us.

Pattern Words
cardiology
cardiopathy
cardiogram
cardiograph
hydropathy
hydroscope
hydrotherapy
hydrothermal
thermostat
thermogenic
thermometer
thermography

Content Words
deuce
velocity
aerobic
diagonally
advantage
boundaries
professionals

Vocabulary Words
arbitrate
arbitrary
perspiration
respiration

1. _____ 2. _____ 3. _____
4. _____ 5. _____ 6. _____
7. _____ 8. _____ 9. _____
10. _____

Name _____

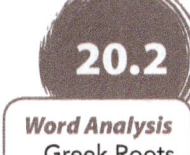

20.2
Word Analysis
Greek Roots

Pattern Words

macrocosm
macroscopic
microcosm
micrograph
microphone
microscopic
monopod
monolithic
monogram
monochromatic
optokinetic
optometry

Greek roots are used to build many words in the English language. A root is the part of a word that gives the basic meaning. Knowledge of word origins helps in building spelling and vocabulary skills.

Write Pattern Words to complete the exercises. Sort by Greek roots.

1.–2. **opto**   3.–4. **macro**   5.–8. **mono**   9.–12. **micro**

1. _____   2. _____
3. _____   4. _____
5. _____   6. _____
7. _____   8. _____
9. _____   10. _____
11. _____   12. _____

Write Content Words to complete the exercises.

13. Badminton is a sport that utilizes l_____, a_____ rackets and a plastic ball with stabilizing feathers called a shuttlecock.

14. One of the r_____ for shuttlecocks is that they be c_____ in shape.

15. The shuttlecock is v_____ back and forth until it drops to one side of the court or the other.

16. In the upcoming months, the players who excel at badminton will be q_____ for their country's Olympic team.

17. Because badminton is a fast-paced game, it is quite e_____ to play.

Content Words

conical
volleyed
qualifying
aluminum
energizing
lightweight
requirements

Vocabulary Words

alteration
altered
inspector
perspective

Challenge Words

_____
_____

badminton

20.2 Vocabulary Greek Roots

Prefix		Root		Suffix	
in-	into	alter	other	-ation	state of
per-	through	spect	look	-ed	makes verbs past tense
				-or	one who
				-ive	inclined to

Pattern Words
macrocosm
macroscopic
microcosm
micrograph
microphone
microscopic
monopod
monolithic
monogram
monochromatic
optokinetic
optometry

Content Words
conical
volleyed
qualifying
aluminum
energizing
lightweight
requirements

Vocabulary Words
alteration
altered
inspector
perspective

Write the Vocabulary Words.

1. _____
2. _____
3. _____
4. _____

Refer to the table to complete the exercises. Match each word to its definition.

_____ 5. inspector — a. changed partly, but not into some other form

_____ 6. perspective — b. the inclination to look at things from one's own point of view

_____ 7. altered — c. the state of changing partly, but not into some other form; modification

_____ 8. alteration — d. one who looks into matters

Write Vocabulary Words to complete the sentences.

9. Jeannie's job as badminton tournament director was challenging. Her first job was to act as the _____ of the court.

10. When she measured the height of the net, Jeannie found it to be six inches too low, so she had to make an _____ to bring the net up to the required height.

11. After she _____ the height of the net, Jeannie went on to check the condition of the rackets and shuttlecocks.

12. From Jeannie's _____, everything was ready for the game to begin.

Choose the best meaning for each underlined word.

13. The <u>monochromatic</u> color scheme looked good on the players.
   ○ very small   ○ consisting of a single color or hue   ○ using initials

14. It would be a <u>monolithic</u> task to defeat the badminton champions.
   ○ huge in proportion   ○ amplifies sound   ○ the universe

Name _____

20.3

Word Study Strategies
Greek Roots

Greek Roots

chrom = color	cosm = universe	gram = write	graph = write
kin = movement	lith = stone	macro = large	metr = measure
micro = small	mono = one	opto = see	phon = sound
pod = foot	scop = see		

Pattern Words
macrocosm
macroscopic
microcosm
micrograph
microphone
microscopic
monopod
monolithic
monogram
monochromatic
optokinetic
optometry

Refer to the Greek roots. Circle the common Greek root in each set of words. Write the root to complete the sentences.

1. optokinetic, optometry

   The Greek root _____ means *see*.

2. macrocosm, macroscopic

   The Greek root _____ means *large*.

3. microcosm, micrograph, microphone, microscopic

   The Greek root _____ means *small*.

4. monopod, monolithic, monogram, monochromatic

   The Greek root _____ means *one*.

Content Words
conical
volleyed
qualifying
aluminum
energizing
lightweight
requirements

Use the information about Greek roots to complete each exercise.
Write the Pattern Words that reflect the combined Greek root meanings.

5. large + universe = _____
6. one + foot = _____
7. small + write = _____
8. see + movement = _____
9. one + stone = _____

Vocabulary Words
alteration
altered
inspector
perspective

Write a Pattern Word with the Greek root shown in parentheses to complete each sentence.

10. (metr) _____ is related to the health of the eyes.
11. (gram) One's _____ consists of one's initials.
12. (phon) A _____ converts sound waves into electrical pulses.
13. (scop) Something that is _____ is visible without magnification.
14. (chrom) A badminton uniform that is only blue in color reflects a _____ color scheme.

Revise and perfect the advertisement from a badminton store. Use proofreading marks. Correctly write the misspelled words.

20.4
Writing Greek Roots

Shop at Badminton Bazaar!

Do you enjoy the fast-paced, enerjizing sport of Badminton? If you do, hurry in to Badminton Bazaar, your headquarters for premium badminton supplies in the tri-county area. we offer great deals on lightwait, alluminum rackets, ranging in price and quality for backyard players as well as serious competitors. Our store also features racket cases, shuttlecocks, shoestrings and apparel.

We carry badminton team jackets in monocromatic shades of blue or green. We can add a monograme to any jacket purchased at our store You can also have an allteration to the sleeve length of of any quallifying jacket at no extra cost. All of our products meet our strict requirments for excellence in in quality

Badminton Bazaar is located at 4703 East Brook Avenue, right next to Eyesight Optomitry. We are open Monday through Saturday from 9 A.M. to 9 P.M. Our expert racket-restringing service is available Saturdays. Orders can be shipped overseas, and we can take orders over the telephone or via fax. From our perspectiv, our service simply cannot be beat! Stop by and give us the chance to be your favorite badminton store!

Proofreading Marks
- ◯ Circle misspellings.
- ≡ Make a capital letter.
- ⊙ Add a period.
- ✀ Delete.
- ∧ Add something.
- / Make a small letter.
- ¶ Make a new paragraph.

Pattern Words
macrocosm
macroscopic
microcosm
micrograph
microphone
microscopic
monopod
monolithic
monogram
monochromatic
optokinetic
optometry

Content Words
conical
volleyed
qualifying
aluminum
energizing
lightweight
requirements

Vocabulary Words
alteration
altered
inspector
perspective

1. _____
2. _____
3. _____
4. _____
5. _____
6. _____
7. _____
8. _____
9. _____
10. _____

Name _____

21.2

Word Analysis
Greek and Latin Roots

Pattern Words

- automobile
- automotive
- autographed
- circumstances
- multilingual
- paralegal
- paramedic
- paramount
- photographer
- semifinal
- televised
- television

Greek and Latin roots and affixes are used to build many words in the English language.

A root is the part of a word that gives the basic meaning. Affixes expand the meaning or function of a word. Knowledge of word origins helps in building spelling and vocabulary skills.

Write Pattern Words to complete the exercises. Sort by Greek and Latin roots.

1. **multi**   2. **circum**   3. **photo**   4. **semi**
5.–6. **tele**   7.–9. **auto**   10.–12. **para**

1. _____   2. _____
3. _____   4. _____
5. _____   6. _____
7. _____   8. _____
9. _____   10. _____
11. _____   12. _____

Write Content Words to complete the exercises.

13. The team f_____ were d_____ the racquetball competition.
14. The sport of racquetball requires speed, racquet control, and quick f_____.
15. The hollow rubber ball did r_____ and r_____ loudly during the match t_____.
16. The rubber ball was i_____ after it bounced off the court and into the thick hedges around the playground.

Content Words

- finalists
- ricochet
- footwork
- tiebreaker
- dominating
- irretrievable
- reverberate

Vocabulary Words

- corporate
- corporation
- expel
- repel

Challenge Words

_____
_____

racquetball

21.2 Vocabulary — Greek and Latin Roots

Prefix		Root		Suffix	
ex-	out of	corpor	body	-ate	to act
re-	back	pel	push	-ation	state of

Write the Vocabulary Words.

1. _____
2. _____
3. _____
4. _____

Refer to the table to complete the exercises. Write the word that is being defined.

5. to push or force out _____
6. to act as one unified body of individuals _____
7. to push, drive back, or exert an opposing force _____
8. the state of a group of individuals acting as one unified body _____

Write Vocabulary Words to complete the sentences.

9. A local _____ donated money for the racquetball competition prize.
10. The _____ decision to donate money was made after the organization realized that many of its employees were competition participants.
11. One participant did _____ a loud breath when the hollow rubber ball ricocheted and hit her in the stomach.
12. She determined to rally back by choosing to _____ the rubber ball forcefully with her racquet as she used quick footwork.

Choose the word that matches each definition.

13. related to speaking several languages
    ○ semifinal ○ televised ○ multilingual
14. the way something happens
    ○ paramedic ○ photographer ○ circumstances
15. greatest
    ○ television ○ paramount ○ automotive

Pattern Words
automobile
automotive
autographed
circumstances
multilingual
paralegal
paramedic
paramount
photographer
semifinal
televised
television

Content Words
finalists
ricochet
footwork
tiebreaker
dominating
irretrievable
reverberate

Vocabulary Words
corporate
corporation
expel
repel

Name _____

21.3

Word Study Strategies
Greek and Latin Roots

Greek and Latin Roots

auto = self	circum = around	fin = end	graph = write
leg = law	lingu = tongue	medic = doctor	mob = move
mot = move	mount = above	multi = many	para = almost
para = by	photo = light	semi = half	stanc = stand
tele = distant	vis = see		

Pattern Words
automobile
automotive
autographed
circumstances
multilingual
paralegal
paramedic
paramount
photographer
semifinal
televised
television

Refer to the Greek and Latin roots. Write the root to complete the sentences.

1. The Greek root _____ means *self*.
2. The Greek root _____ means *distant*.
3. The Greek root _____ means *light*.
4. The Greek root _____ means *almost*.
5. The Latin root _____ means *by*.
6. The Latin root _____ means *around*.
7. The Latin root _____ means *half*.
8. The Latin root _____ means *many*.

Content Words
finalists
ricochet
footwork
tiebreaker
dominating
irretrievable
reverberate

Use the information about Greek and Latin roots to complete each exercise. Write the Pattern Words that reflect the combined root meanings.

9. almost + doctor = _____
10. light + write = _____
11. many + tongue = _____
12. almost + law = _____
13. self + write = _____
14. by + above = _____
15. distant + see = _____ _____
16. self + move = _____ _____

Vocabulary Words
corporate
corporation
expel
repel

Write the missing root or affix to complete each underlined Pattern or Vocabulary Word. Locate and circle the Content Words.

17. The <u>photo_____</u> took a picture of some of the finalists during the <u>semi_____</u> match.

18. The members of the <u>corpor_____</u> made a <u>corpor_____</u> decision about the <u>circum_____</u> involving the tournament tiebreaker.

Spelling Plus Grade 6

Lionel wrote a letter to the editor of his local community newspaper. The editor thought that Lionel's concern was of great importance and decided to publish the letter. Read the letter and write the missing words.

21.4

Writing Greek and Latin Roots

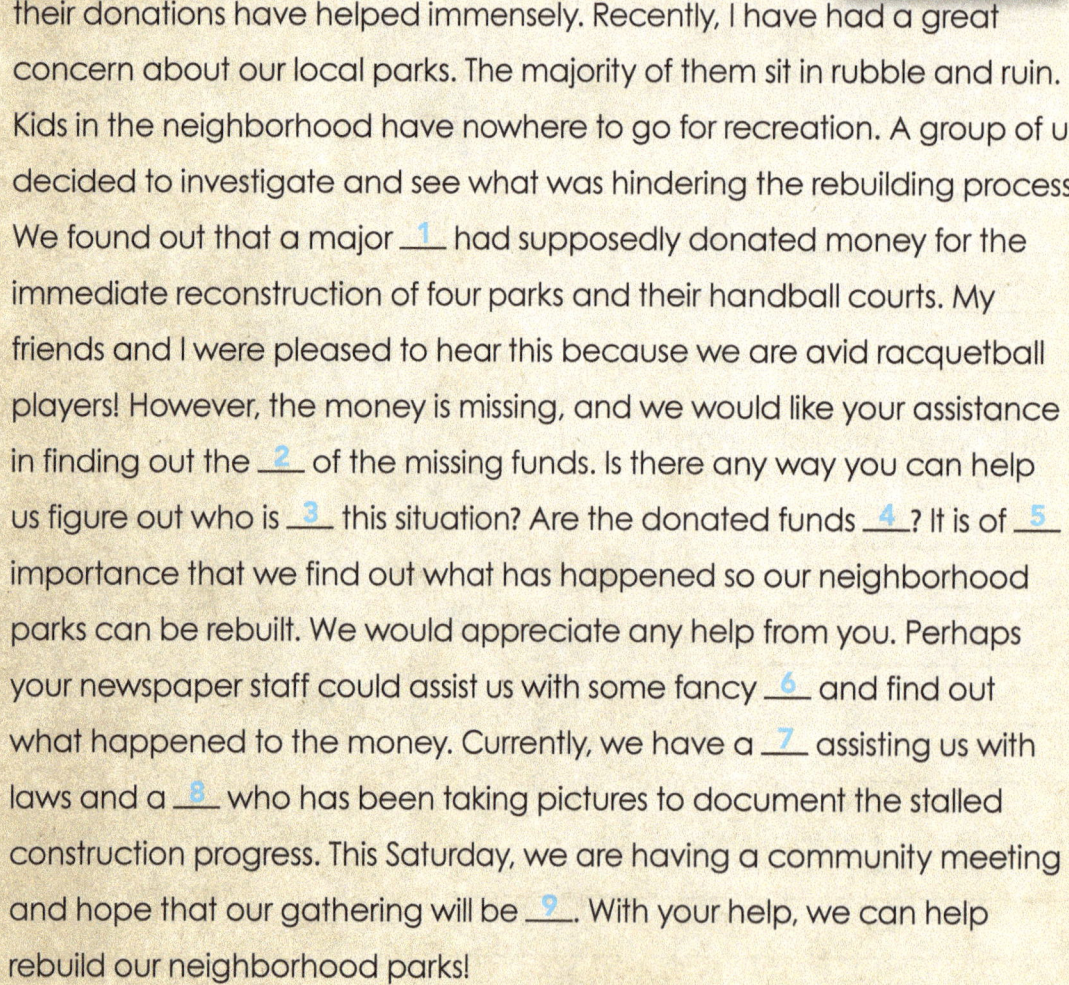

Dear Editor,

Since the passing of Hurricane Yolanda, cleaning teams, construction crews, and numerous volunteers have effortlessly given of their time. Many businesses have come forward and donated funds to help rebuild our community, and their donations have helped immensely. Recently, I have had a great concern about our local parks. The majority of them sit in rubble and ruin. Kids in the neighborhood have nowhere to go for recreation. A group of us decided to investigate and see what was hindering the rebuilding process. We found out that a major __1__ had supposedly donated money for the immediate reconstruction of four parks and their handball courts. My friends and I were pleased to hear this because we are avid racquetball players! However, the money is missing, and we would like your assistance in finding out the __2__ of the missing funds. Is there any way you can help us figure out who is __3__ this situation? Are the donated funds __4__? It is of __5__ importance that we find out what has happened so our neighborhood parks can be rebuilt. We would appreciate any help from you. Perhaps your newspaper staff could assist us with some fancy __6__ and find out what happened to the money. Currently, we have a __7__ assisting us with laws and a __8__ who has been taking pictures to document the stalled construction progress. This Saturday, we are having a community meeting and hope that our gathering will be __9__. With your help, we can help rebuild our neighborhood parks!

Sincerely,
Lionel Duncan, age 12

Pattern Words
automobile
automotive
autographed
circumstances
multilingual
paralegal
paramedic
paramount
photographer
semifinal
televised
television

Content Words
finalists
ricochet
footwork
tiebreaker
dominating
irretrievable
reverberate

Vocabulary Words
corporate
corporation
expel
repel

1. _____
2. _____
3. _____
4. _____
5. _____
6. _____
7. _____
8. _____
9. _____

Name _____

22.2
Word Analysis
Hard and Soft c, g

Pattern Words

gauge
original
cultural
disguise
ethnicity
garages
certainly
languages
successful
customary
occurrence
knowledgeable

Write Pattern Words to complete the exercises.
Sort the hard and soft **c** and **g** words.

1.–2. Both hard and soft **c**   3.–4. Only hard **c**   5.–6. Only soft **c**
7.–9. Both hard and soft **g**   10. Only hard **g**   11.–12. Only soft **g**

1. _____ 2. _____
3. _____ 4. _____
5. _____ 6. _____
7. _____ 8. _____
9. _____ 10. _____
11. _____ 12. _____

Write Content Words to complete the exercises.

13. Table tennis is both a competitive and r_____ sport in many countries.
14. Each player a_____ hitting the hollow, lightweight ball, which is made of c_____, across the table.
15. In the competitive sport of table tennis, c_____ should have quick r_____.
16. Competitors should also have good hand-eye c_____ and the ability to have focused c_____.

Content Words

celluloid
reflexes
alternates
contenders
recreational
coordination
concentration

Vocabulary Words

dialect
lecture
composition
disposition

Challenge Words

_____
_____

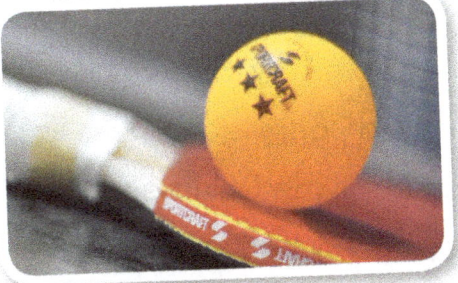

table tennis

22.2
Vocabulary
Hard and Soft c, g

Prefix		Root		Suffix	
dia-	across	lect	gather	-ure	process
com-	together	posit	place	-ion	state of
dis-	away				

Write the Vocabulary Words.

1. _____   2. _____
3. _____   4. _____

Refer to the table to complete the exercises. Match each word to its definition.

_____ 5. dialect   a. a state of thoroughly placing together; construction of

_____ 6. composition   b. a type of language spoken across a specific area or region

_____ 7. lecture   c. a state of certain behavior when placed under specific circumstances; personality

_____ 8. disposition   d. a presentation of gathered information

Write Vocabulary Words to complete the sentences.

9. Brita attended a _____ on the history of table tennis at the university hall.

10. Brita easily understood the Mandarin _____ that the lecturer was speaking.

11. The lecturer's _____ was cordial, and he displayed a genuine smile.

12. After the lecture, Brita returned to her dormitory room and wrote a _____ about the origin of table tennis.

13. Brita felt confident that her attendance at the Chinese athlete's _____ would greatly benefit her report.

14. In her report, Brita explained that the _____ of celluloid balls was mainly of sulfuric acid, cellulose, and camphor.

Pattern Words
gauge
original
cultural
disguise
ethnicity
garages
certainly
languages
successful
customary
occurrence
knowledgeable

Content Words
celluloid
reflexes
alternates
contenders
recreational
coordination
concentration

Vocabulary Words
dialect
lecture
composition
disposition

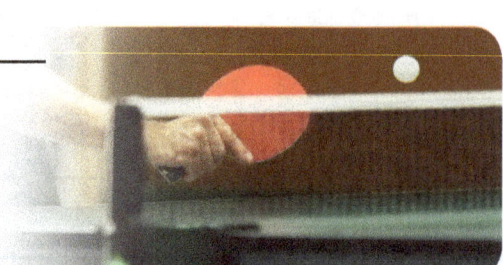

Name _____

22.3

Word Study Strategies
Hard and Soft c, g

Write each list word from the pronunciation shown.

1. /'gāj/ _____
2. /dis 'gīz/ _____
3. /'dī ə lekt/ _____
4. /gə 'rä jəz/ _____
5. /'sel yə loid/ _____
6. /ə 'kûr ənts/ _____
7. /'sûr tən lē/ _____
8. /sək 'ses fəl/ _____
9. /eth 'ni sə tē/ _____
10. /'rē flek səz/ _____
11. /'no lij ə bəl/ _____
12. /'kul chə rəl/ _____
13. /'lang gwi jəz/ _____
14. /kom pə 'zi shən/ _____
15. /kō ôr də 'nā shən/ _____
16. /re krē 'ā shə nəl/ _____

Pattern Words
gauge
original
cultural
disguise
ethnicity
garages
certainly
languages
successful
customary
occurrence
knowledgeable

Content Words
celluloid
reflexes
alternates
contenders
recreational
coordination
concentration

Vocabulary Words
dialect
lecture
composition
disposition

Use the meaning of each related form to write a list word.

17. An **alternative** is another possibility.

    Something **alternating** is fluctuating back and forth.

    Something that _____ follows in succession or fluctuates.

18. An **origin** is the source from which something develops.

    An **originator** is the inventor of something.

    Something that is _____ is first, innovative, or inventive.

19. A **lectern** is a reading stand for a speaker's notes.

    A **lectionary** is a list or book of Scripture readings.

    A _____ is a presentation of gathered information.

20. A **custom** is a tradition or habit.

    Something **customized** is changed to better suit one's standards.

    Something _____ is usual or common.

A synonym is a word that means the same or almost the same as another word. Read the speech. Write a list word that is a synonym for each underlined word. Use the Spelling Dictionary.

22.4

Writing
Hard and Soft c, g

The Health Benefits of Sports

Sluggishness, slothfulness, and idleness—sound like your idea of fun? **Definitely** not! One should not choose to be inactive. The Lord created our bodies, and we should be responsible and wisely take care of them. This oral and written composition will convince you that exercise and a healthy diet are great ways to take care of our bodies.

Using a sport as a form of exercise is not an **innovative** idea. Many professional athletes enjoy their involvement in sports even when it is in a casual, **fun** setting. An example of this is the sport of table tennis. Table tennis is a popular, cultural sport in Asia with many **competitors**. One may laugh at the idea of hitting a hollow **plastic** ball as a sport, but playing table tennis can increase one's heart rate, burn calories, and tone arm muscles.

Many sports help to enhance one's **reactions** and **dexterity**. Sports can also improve one's processes of **thought**. Be sure to **judge** whether or not the level of exercise activity is appropriate as you are participating in the sport.

Being **wise** about the health benefits of sports will ensure a healthy lifestyle. Regular exercise will help one's **personality** be positive. If you implement what has been suggested, you will have **favorable** results!

Pattern Words
gauge
original
cultural
disguise
ethnicity
garages
certainly
languages
successful
customary
occurrence
knowledgeable

Content Words
celluloid
reflexes
alternates
contenders
recreational
coordination
concentration

Vocabulary Words
dialect
lecture
composition
disposition

1. _____
2. _____
3. _____
4. _____
5. _____
6. _____
7. _____
8. _____
9. _____
10. _____
11. _____
12. _____

Name _____

23.2

Word Analysis
Variant Consonant Spellings

Pattern Words

visual
insured
laughter
advisable
brochure
machinery
emphasize
measurable
phenomenal
architectural
roughhousing
advertisement

Write Pattern Words to complete the exercises.
Sort the variant consonant spellings.

1.–4. /f/ spelled *gh* or *ph*   5. /k/ spelled *ch*
6.–8. /sh/ spelled *ch* or *s*   9.–10. /z/ spelled *s*
11.–12. /zh/ spelled *s*

1. _____   2. _____
3. _____   4. _____
5. _____   6. _____
7. _____   8. _____
9. _____   10. _____
11. _____   12. _____

Write Content Words to complete the exercises.

13. In a r_____ field-hockey game, there are two periods of thirty-five minutes with a halftime of five minutes.

14. C_____ with opponents can cause i_____.

15. Ice hockey is a fast-paced, a_____ sport.

16. During s_____ in a hockey game, it is important for athletes to replenish fluids.

17. A field-hockey team has eleven players in four p_____ whereas ice hockey has six players in three positions.

18. Athletes have their own training regimen to develop m_____ strength and endurance.

Content Words

injuries
collisions
positions
muscular
regulation
stoppages
aggressive

Vocabulary Words

innocence
innocently
absolution
resolution

Challenge Words

_____
_____

field hockey

23.2 Vocabulary — Variant Consonant Spellings

Prefix		Root		Suffix	
in-	not	noc	harm	-ence	state of
ab-	from	solut	set free	-ent	inclined to
in-	back			-ly	forms an adverb from an adjective
				-ion	state of

Pattern Words
visual
insured
laughter
advisable
brochure
machinery
emphasize
measurable
phenomenal
architectural
roughhousing
advertisement

Content Words
injuries
collisions
positions
muscular
regulation
stoppages
aggressive

Vocabulary Words
innocence
innocently
absolution
resolution

Write the Vocabulary Words.

1. _____
2. _____
3. _____
4. _____

Refer to the table to complete the exercises. Write the word that is being defined.

5. not inclined to cause harm _____
6. state of being set free from something; determination _____
7. state of causing no harm; blamelessness or guiltlessness _____
8. state of being set free from blame or guilt _____

Write Vocabulary Words to complete the sentences.

9. The player _____ made a bad pass that caused the puck to enter his own goal.
10. The player's _____ was not believed by his coach who sent him to the bench.
11. Although the player had made a bad pass that led to the other team scoring first, the player achieved _____ when his team scored the next two goals.
12. The player's _____ to not repeat his mistake led him to be the most valuable player at the end of the season.

Choose the word that matches each definition.

13. remarkable
    ○ roughhousing
    ○ phenomenal
    ○ positions

14. pamphlet
    ○ brochure
    ○ stoppages
    ○ injuries

Name _____

23.3
Word Study Strategies
Variant Consonant Spellings

Write each list word from the pronunciation shown.

1. /'laf tûr/ _____
2. /fi 'no mə nəl/ _____
3. /'me zhə rə bəl/ _____
4. /'vi zhə wəl/ _____
5. /in 'shoord/ _____
6. /ad vûr 'tīz mənt/ _____

Listen to the sound of the underlined letter or letters. Fill in the circle in front of the word that has the same sound.

7. p<u>h</u>enomenal
   ○ brochure
   ○ laughter
   ○ visual

8. adverti<u>s</u>ement
   ○ advisable
   ○ architectural
   ○ insured

9. rou<u>gh</u>housing
   ○ machinery
   ○ measurable
   ○ emphasize

10. ma<u>ch</u>inery
    ○ emphasize
    ○ brochure
    ○ roughhousing

11. vi<u>s</u>ual
    ○ measurable
    ○ advertisement
    ○ phenomenal

12. in<u>s</u>ured
    ○ machinery
    ○ laughter
    ○ advisable

13. advi<u>s</u>able
    ○ measurable
    ○ phenomenal
    ○ advertisement

14. lau<u>gh</u>ter
    ○ machinery
    ○ roughhousing
    ○ architectural

15. bro<u>ch</u>ure
    ○ visual
    ○ emphasize
    ○ insured

Pattern Words
visual
insured
laughter
advisable
brochure
machinery
emphasize
measurable
phenomenal
architectural
roughhousing
advertisement

Content Words
injuries
collisions
positions
muscular
regulation
stoppages
aggressive

Vocabulary Words
innocence
innocently
absolution
resolution

A sentence fragment is an incomplete sentence that does not express a complete thought. A fragment is missing the subject, predicate, or both.

Write a complete sentence from each fragment. Circle the list words.

16. The aggressive hockey players. _____
_____

17. Innocently hit the puck into the opponent's goal. _____
_____

18. Made a resolution. _____
_____

19. A regulation hockey puck. _____
_____

Read the facts about field hockey and ice hockey. Knowing the facts about something helps in forming a personal opinion. Write list words to complete the paragraphs.

23.4

Writing Variant Consonant Spellings

Hockey

Two variations of hockey—field hockey and ice hockey—are played by men and women in many countries. Hockey is a sport that builds leadership and negotiation skills and requires excellent hand-eye coordination, strength, and endurance. Although similar, field hockey and ice hockey are separate sports.

Field hockey is played outdoors on a field. Eleven players occupy four p_____—forward, halfback, fullback, and goalie. Players use a wooden stick that is curved at one end to hit a ball into the opponent's goal. The ball has a circumference of about nine inches and weighs less than six ounces. Field hockey is played as an amateur sport as well as a professional sport in many countries. In the United States, field hockey is primarily played by women.

Ice hockey is a fast-paced game usually played in an indoor rink. Players wear a helmet and use a hockey stick to hit a puck into the opponent's goal. A r_____ puck is made from black rubber, is one inch thick, and is three inches in diameter. Six athletic, m_____ players occupy three positions—forward, defender, and goalie. Ice hockey requires players to be adept at ice-skating. Players must be able to accelerate, maintain balance, stop quickly, and change direction abruptly. In essence, players must be able to skate as naturally as they walk. Because ice hockey is fast paced, mental agility is necessary since plays need to be memorized. It is imperative that players think and react quickly. Men's ice hockey is an a_____ sport in which players are often r_____ and causing i_____. In women's ice hockey, c_____ occur, but overall, the sport is much less hostile than men's ice hockey.

Pattern Words
visual
insured
laughter
advisable
brochure
machinery
emphasize
measurable
phenomenal
architectural
roughhousing
advertisement

Content Words
injuries
collisions
positions
muscular
regulation
stoppages
aggressive

Vocabulary Words
innocence
innocently
absolution
resolution

Which variation of hockey would you rather play? Why? Write your opinion in complete sentences.

_____
_____
_____

Name _____

Review Chapters 19–23
Chapter 19

Pattern Words

Chapter 19 Greek Roots	Chapter 20 Greek Roots	Chapter 21 Greek and Latin Roots	Chapter 22 Hard and Soft c, g	Chapter 23 Variant Consonant Spellings
cardiology	macrocosm	automobile	gauge	visual
cardiopathy	macroscopic	automotive	original	insured
cardiogram	microcosm	autographed	cultural	laughter
cardiograph	micrograph	circumstances	disguise	advisable
hydropathy	microphone	multilingual	ethnicity	brochure
hydroscope	microscopic	paralegal	garages	machinery
hydrotherapy	monopod	paramedic	certainly	emphasize
hydrothermal	monolithic	paramount	languages	measurable
thermostat	monogram	photographer	successful	phenomenal
thermogenic	monochromatic	semifinal	customary	architectural
thermometer	optokinetic	televised	occurrence	roughhousing
thermography	optometry	television	knowledgeable	advertisement

Content Words

deuce	conical	finalists	celluloid	injuries
velocity	volleyed	ricochet	reflexes	collisions
aerobic	qualifying	footwork	alternates	positions
diagonally	aluminum	tiebreaker	contenders	muscular
advantage	energizing	dominating	recreational	regulation
boundaries	lightweight	irretrievable	coordination	stoppages
professionals	requirements	reverberate	concentration	aggressive

Vocabulary Words

arbitrate	alteration	corporate	dialect	innocence
arbitrary	altered	corporation	lecture	innocently
perspiration	inspector	expel	composition	absolution
respiration	perspective	repel	disposition	resolution

Read Chapter 19 Pattern Words. Follow the directions given.

1. Place a check mark next to the words with the roots **cardio** and **hydro**.

2. Circle the words with the roots **gram**, **graph**, and **meter**.

3. Underline the words with the roots **stat**, **gen**, and **path**.

4. Write the words that are both checkmarked and circled.

   _____   _____

© Spelling Plus Grade 6

93

Write words from Chapter 20 that reflect the combined Greek root meanings.

24.2

Review Chapters 19–23
Chapters 20–21

Greek Roots

chrom = color	cosm = universe	gram = write	graph = write
kin = movement	lith = stone	macro = large	metr = measure
micro = small	mono = one	opto = see	phon = sound
pod = foot	scop = see		

macrocosm
macroscopic
microcosm
micrograph
microphone
microscopic
monopod
monolithic
monogram
monochromatic
optokinetic
optometry

1. one + color = _____
2. small + sound = _____
3. small + see = _____
4. see + measure = _____
5. one + stone = _____
6. large + see = _____
7. small + write = _____
8. one + write = _____
9. one + foot = _____
10. small + universe = _____
11. large + universe = _____
12. see + movement = _____

Write the words in the shape boxes. Each blue shaded portion indicates the Greek root of the word. Each orange shaded portion indicates the Latin root of the word.

automobile
automotive
autographed
circumstances
multilingual
paralegal
paramedic
paramount
photographer
semifinal
televised
television

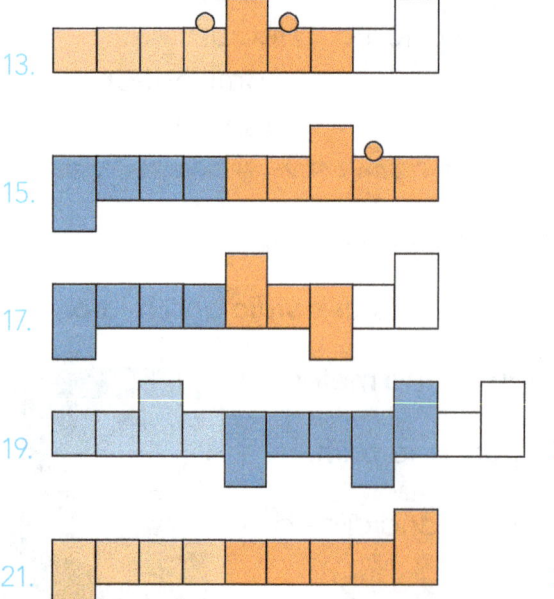
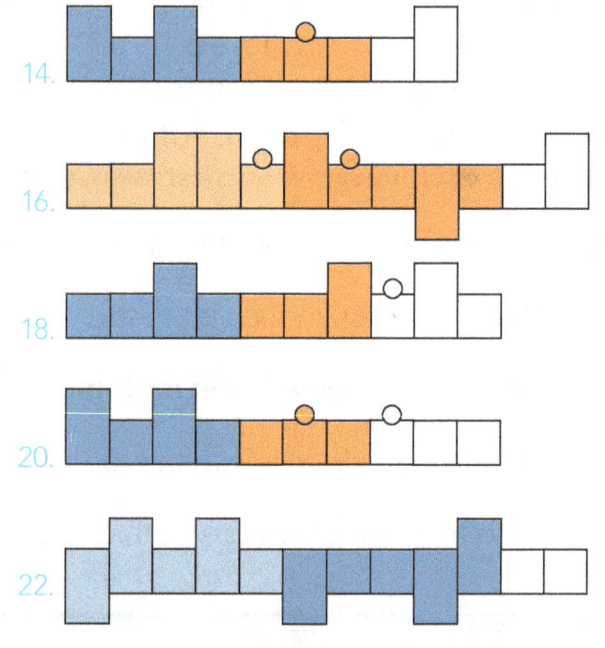

13.
14.
15.
16.
17.
18.
19.
20.
21.
22.

Name _____

24.3

Read each word. Decide if it is spelled correctly or incorrectly. Fill in the circle. Write each word correctly.

Review Chapters 19–23
Chapters 22–23

	Correct	Incorrect	
1. original	○	○	_____
2. cultureal	○	○	_____
3. garajes	○	○	_____
4. languajes	○	○	_____
5. customerry	○	○	_____
6. guage	○	○	_____
7. disguise	○	○	_____
8. ethnisity	○	○	_____
9. successful	○	○	_____
10. occurence	○	○	_____
11. knowledgable	○	○	_____
12. certainly	○	○	_____

gauge
original
cultural
disguise
ethnicity
garages
certainly
languages
successful
customary
occurrence
knowledgeable

Find the words in the word search. Circle them and write them on the lines. The words go across, down, diagonally, and backwards. Some of the words share letters. One list word is not used.

visual
insured
laughter
advisable
brochure
machinery
emphasize
measurable
phenomenal
architectural
roughhousing
advertisement

b	y	c	f	t	f	l	a	u	g	h	t	e	r	l	d
r	e	m	p	h	a	s	i	z	e	n	g	r	r	b	e
m	e	a	s	u	r	a	b	l	e	o	r	u	e	r	r
w	d	x	s	l	a	n	e	m	o	n	e	h	p	x	u
l	a	i	e	m	o	n	e	h	p	u	t	c	i	c	s
a	v	m	a	c	h	i	n	e	r	y	n	o	h	h	n
e	g	n	i	s	u	o	h	h	g	u	o	r	c	u	i
j	l	a	r	u	t	a	d	v	i	s	a	b	l	e	r
r	a	r	c	h	i	t	e	c	t	u	r	a	l	e	x

_____ _____ _____
_____ _____ _____
_____ _____ _____
_____ _____ _____

Read the article. Unscramble each Content Word and write it correctly.

24.4
Review Chapters 19–23
Content and Vocabulary Words

Racket and Paddle Sports

Racket and paddle sports are both **alrenatiocre** and professional sports. These **oicbaer** sports are exhilarating and **ringgienez** to play. Tennis and badminton involve returning a ball or shuttlecock over a net. These sports are often played with **muminalu** rackets. The goal of both games is to make a shot that is **leirievrreabt** by the other team.

Other sports use paddles or sticks instead of rackets. **Ceonentrsd** in table tennis play with a **igwethtligh** ball and paddles. Hockey players use hockey sticks to propel a ball or a puck at a high **ctyveloi**. Racket and paddle sports can be challenging and **agsivresge** sports to play.

deuce
velocity
aerobic
aluminum
energizing
lightweight
dominating
irretrievable
reverberate
alternates
contenders
recreational
regulation
stoppages
aggressive

1. _____ 2. _____ 3. _____
4. _____ 5. _____ 6. _____
7. _____ 8. _____ 9. _____

arbitrate
arbitrary
perspiration
altered
inspector
perspective
corporate
corporation
expel
lecture
composition
disposition
innocence
innocently
absolution

	A	B	C	D	E	F	G
1	per-	in-	arbitr	spect	lect	solut	-ed
2	com-	ex-	spir	corpor	posit	-ate	-or
3	dis-	ab-	alter	pel	noc	-ion	-ive
4	-ence	-ation	-ary	re-	-ly	dia-	-ent

Find the coordinates given. Write the Vocabulary Words.

10. A1 + C2 + B4 = _____
11. D2 + F2 = _____
12. B2 + D3 = _____
13. C3 + G1 = _____
14. B1 + E3 + A4 = _____
15. B1 + D1 + G2 = _____
16. A3 + E2 + F3 = _____
17. B3 + F1 + F3 = _____

Name _____

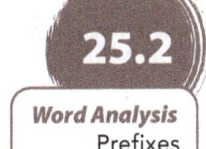

25.2
Word Analysis
Prefixes

Pattern Words
- antistress
- antibiotics
- disability
- dislocation
- embodied
- embraced
- immovable
- improvement
- invariably
- incredulous
- midsole
- midfield

A prefix is a word part that is added to the beginning of a root or a root with a suffix.

Write Pattern Words to complete the exercises. Sort the words according to their spelling when adding the prefix. The prefixes are anti-, dis-, em-, im-, in-, and mid-.

1.–2. **mid-**   3.–4. **dis-**   5.–6. **in-**   7.–8. **anti-**
9.–10. **im-**   11.–12. **em-**

1. _____   2. _____
3. _____   4. _____
5. _____   6. _____
7. _____   8. _____
9. _____   10. _____
11. _____   12. _____

Write Content Words to complete the exercises.

13. Sprints or dashes are the shortest distance running events in track-and-field competition. Runners may start by c_____ in starting blocks.

14. Each s_____ in the 400-meter event begins in his or her own lane on a m_____ track.

15. Sprinters run c_____ around the track, beginning s_____ at the starting signal.

16. Running short distances requires runners to stay on the balls of their feet and to e_____ their stride.

17. One of the c_____ of the 1924 Olympics was a Christian sprinter named Eric Liddell.

Content Words
- sprinter
- elongate
- multilane
- crouching
- champions
- simultaneously
- counterclockwise

Vocabulary Words
- abruptly
- disruption
- revived
- vivacious

Challenge Words

_____
_____

short-distance running

Spelling Plus Grade 6   97

25.2 Vocabulary Prefixes

Prefix		Root		Suffix	
ab-	away	rupt	break	-ly	forms an adverb from an adjective
dis-	off	viv	life	-ion	state of
re-	again			-ed	makes verbs past tense
				-acious	quality of

Pattern Words
antistress
antibiotics
disability
dislocation
embodied
embraced
immovable
improvement
invariably
incredulous
midsole
midfield

Content Words
sprinter
elongate
multilane
crouching
champions
simultaneously
counterclockwise

Vocabulary Words
abruptly
disruption
revived
vivacious

Write the Vocabulary Words.

1. _____
2. _____
3. _____
4. _____

Refer to the table to complete the exercises. Write the word that is being defined.

5. in a sudden breaking away; suddenly _____
6. brought back to life _____
7. having the quality of liveliness; perky; lively _____
8. the state of breaking something apart or interrupting _____

Write Vocabulary Words to complete the sentences.

9. At the track meet, Eva competed in the 200- and 400-meter races. Her competitors enjoyed meeting her because she has a _____ personality.

10. Before the start of the 400-meter race, Eva _____ stopped stretching and grasped her calf.

11. A slight cramp in her leg had caused a momentary _____ in her preparation for the race.

12. Eva massaged the cramp and drank some water, which _____ her in time for the race.

Choose the best meaning for each underlined word.

13. Marco <u>invariably</u> arrived early for practice.
    ○ always   ○ never   ○ soon

14. He <u>embodied</u> the qualities of a dedicated sprinter.
    ○ embraced   ○ personified   ○ revived

98

Name _____

25.3
Word Study Strategies
Prefixes

A prefix is an affix. Affixes expand the meaning or function of a word.

Prefixes
- anti- = against
- em- = put into
- in- = in, not, into
- dis- = not, off, apart
- im- = in, not, into
- mid- = middle

Pattern Words
antistress
antibiotics
disability
dislocation
embodied
embraced
immovable
improvement
invariably
incredulous
midsole
midfield

Write the Pattern Word that matches each definition.

1. not able to be moved _____
2. not varying; always _____
3. placed into one's arms _____
4. the middle of the field _____
5. that which works against stress _____
6. not inclined to believe; unbelieving _____
7. the middle part of a shoe's sole _____
8. the condition of not being completely able-bodied _____

Sentence fluency can be improved by combining short, choppy sentences that share the same subject.

Combine two sentences to form one sentence having a compound predicate. Use a coordinating conjunction as needed. The first one is done for you.

9. We started to run simultaneously. We finished at different times.
   We started to run simultaneously but finished at different times.

10. Lucas begins the race by crouching. Lucas runs counterclockwise.
    _____

11. Sue was incredulous at her finishing time. Sue noticed improvement.
    _____

12. The champions gathered in the midfield. The champions embraced their coach.
    _____

Content Words
sprinter
elongate
multilane
crouching
champions
simultaneously
counterclockwise

Vocabulary Words
abruptly
disruption
revived
vivacious

A biography is a written account of someone's life. Read the biography about Eric Liddell, an Olympic champion who was a missionary. Write the list words that could replace the bold words in each sentence. Use the Spelling Dictionary as a reference.

25.4

Writing Prefixes

The Flying Scotsman

Eric Liddell was born in China on January 16, 1902. His parents, Rev. and Mrs. James Dunlop Liddell, were Scottish missionaries. Eric lived in China until he was five years old. Then, the Liddells returned to Scotland where Eric Liddell was enrolled at Eltham College, a boarding school for missionaries' children. It was at school that Eric became a **short-distance runner**¹ and was known as the Flying Scotsman, the fastest man in Scotland. Liddell became one of the **winners**² of short-distance events in both England and Scotland. Soon, he began preparing to run in the 1924 Olympic Games.

Although training for the Olympics occupied much of his time, Liddell was speaking out for his faith **at the same time**³. He **personified**⁴ many Christ-like qualities including a kind spirit. Eric Liddell **always**⁵ showed compassion and kindness to his competitors.

In 1981, a film called *Chariots of Fire* was made about Liddell's participation in the 1924 Olympic Games. In the film, Liddell's firm Christian faith was evident. Eric refused to take part in sprinting events that were held on Sunday, a day of worship. He only ran in races held on weekdays. This decision left many fellow runners **unbelieving**⁶ that someone would put his faith ahead of his sport, but Eric was **not able to be moved**⁷ in his stand for his Christian faith.

After winning a gold medal in the Olympics, Eric Liddell returned to missionary work in China. Eric Liddell said, "We are all missionaries. Wherever we go, we either bring people nearer to Christ, or we repel them from Christ."

Pattern Words
antistress
antibiotics
disability
dislocation
embodied
embraced
immovable
improvement
invariably
incredulous
midsole
midfield

Content Words
sprinter
elongate
multilane
crouching
champions
simultaneously
counterclockwise

Vocabulary Words
abruptly
disruption
revived
vivacious

1. _____ 2. _____
3. _____ 4. _____
5. _____ 6. _____ 7. _____

Name _____

26.2
Word Analysis
Prefixes

Pattern Words

mistreated
mismanaged
multicultural
multitalented
postexercise
postoperative
proactive
prolonged
superathlete
supereffective
underestimate
undernourished

Content Words

fatigue
stamina
disciplined
surpassed
conditioning
strategizing
dehydration

Vocabulary Words

duration
enduring
opposed
supposing

A prefix is a word part that is added to the beginning of a root or a root with a suffix.

Write Pattern Words to complete the exercises. Sort the words according to their spelling when adding the prefix. The prefixes are *mis-*, *multi-*, *post-*, *pro-*, *super-*, and *under-*.

1.–2. **pro-**   3.–4. **multi-**   5.–6. **under-**
7.–8. **mis-**   9.–10. **super-**   11.–12. **post-**

1. _____   2. _____
3. _____   4. _____
5. _____   6. _____
7. _____   8. _____
9. _____   10. _____
11. _____   12. _____

Write Content Words to complete the exercises.

13. Ross d_____ himself to run at least thirty minutes at a time while training for the race.

14. To avoid d_____, runners should drink plenty of water daily.

15. A symptom of dehydration is extreme f_____.

16. Coaches are often s_____ with long-distance runners in order to increase their performance.

17. C_____ is important to develop s_____ before competing in a long-distance race such as a marathon.

18. Runners who have s_____ their own personal record are ecstatic.

Challenge Words

_____
_____

long-distance running

101

26.2 Vocabulary Prefixes

Prefix		Root		Suffix	
en-	in	dur	lasting	-ation	state of
op-	against	pos	put	-ing	continuous action
sup-	under			-ed	makes verbs past tense

Pattern Words
mistreated
mismanaged
multicultural
multitalented
postexercise
postoperative
proactive
prolonged
superathlete
supereffective
underestimate
undernourished

Write the Vocabulary Words.

1. _____ 2. _____
3. _____ 4. _____

Refer to the table to complete the exercises. Match each word to its definition.

_____ 5. opposed   a. to last without quitting
_____ 6. enduring   b. to continually put one's thoughts under an assumption
_____ 7. supposing   c. the state of or the period of time for which something lasts
_____ 8. duration   d. to have been against something; was against

Content Words
fatigue
stamina
disciplined
surpassed
conditioning
strategizing
dehydration

Write Vocabulary Words to complete the sentences.

9. Although Jaye has recently started running, she is not _____ to training for a marathon.

10. She will begin conditioning in order to build the stamina that is needed for the _____ of the race.

11. Jaye knows that a marathon is a tremendous challenge and is _____ the training to accomplish the feat.

12. Since she is training hard, Jaye is _____ that she will accept the challenge to complete the race and not be a runner who drops out.

Vocabulary Words
duration
enduring
opposed
supposing

Choose the best meaning for each word.

13. surpassed
   ○ exceeded
   ○ excited
   ○ exceptional

14. conditioning
   ○ a reading skill
   ○ a carving technique
   ○ a training process

102

Name _____

26.3

Word Study Strategies
Prefixes

A prefix is an affix. Affixes expand the meaning or function of a word.

Prefixes
mis- = wrong, bad
post- = after
super- = more, better, higher
multi- = many, much
pro- = forward, toward
under- = below, less than

Pattern Words
mistreated
mismanaged
multicultural
multitalented
postexercise
postoperative
proactive
prolonged
superathlete
supereffective
underestimate
undernourished

Write the Pattern Word that matches each definition.

1. acting in anticipation toward future problems _____
2. many abilities _____
3. to have handled wrongly _____
4. to estimate less than the actual size or amount _____
5. an athlete with more skills and abilities than other athletes _____
6. to have treated badly _____
7. after an operation _____
8. many cultures _____
9. better results than anticipated _____
10. a routine after a workout _____

Content Words
fatigue
stamina
disciplined
surpassed
conditioning
strategizing
dehydration

Write a word that is a related form of each group of words.

11. surpassing, unsurpassed, surpassable, _____
12. undisciplined, disciplining, disciplinary, _____
13. nourishment, malnourish, nourishing, _____
14. hydrate, hydration, dehydrated, _____
15. prolonging, prolong, longingly, _____
16. endure, endurance, duration, _____
17. opposed, supposed, opposition, _____
18. athleticism, athletics, athlete, _____
19. fatiguingly, fatigues, fatigability, _____
20. conditioned, unconditional, conditions, _____

Vocabulary Words
duration
enduring
opposed
supposing

Kirk read an article about long-distance running. He wrote an informative summary about the sport. Use proofreading marks to identify mistakes in his paragraphs. Correctly write the misspelled words.

26.4
Writing Prefixes

Long-Distance Running

A long-distance run is any distance over one and a a half miles. common long-distance running competitions are the 5K, 10K, and Marathon   Triathlons and decathlons also include a long-distance running event. Cross-Country running refers to running that is not on a road or track, but rather through the woods and over rolling hills. Competitive cross-country races can be from one and a half miles to nine miles. Disiplined athletes who participate in long-distance running condition themselves in order to increase their stamanna and performance. Runners who not proactiv in devising a plan for condishioning run the risk of fatiege and injury. It is essential for runners to maintain a proper workout that involves a warm-up, a steady pace, and postexcercize activities. proper food and liquid intake also a vital part of an exercise regimen in order to not become undernureshed or dehydrated. To avoid dehidration, runners should adequately drink fluids before, during, and after exercise

Long-distance running is a popular, universal, and multeculchural sport. Thousands of athletes participate in long-distance running competitions each year. An athlete can run wherever there is a road, a trail, or a path. There is no need for special equipment other than comfortable clothes and good running shoes. From kenya to California, Athletes participate in in long-distance running both competitively and leisurely.

Proofreading Marks
- ◯ Circle misspellings.
- ≡ Make a capital letter.
- ⊙ Add a period.
- ꝑ Delete.
- ∧ Add something.
- / Make a small letter.
- ¶ Make a new paragraph.

Pattern Words
mistreated
mismanaged
multicultural
multitalented
postexercise
postoperative
proactive
prolonged
superathlete
supereffective
underestimate
undernourished

Content Words
fatigue
stamina
disciplined
surpassed
conditioning
strategizing
dehydration

Vocabulary Words
duration
enduring
opposed
supposing

1. _____
2. _____
3. _____
4. _____
5. _____
6. _____
7. _____
8. _____
9. _____

Name _____

27.2 Word Analysis — Suffixes

Pattern Words
- dosage
- storage
- percentage
- availability
- impossibility
- responsibility
- statistically
- immediately
- scholarship
- sportsmanship
- achievement
- arrangement

A **suffix** is a word part that is added to the ending of a root or a root with a prefix.

Write Pattern Words to complete the exercises. Sort the words according to their spelling when adding the suffix. The suffixes are -age, -ility, -ly, -ment, and -ship.

1.–3. Words that keep **silent e**   4.–7. Words that do not change
8.–10. Words that drop **-le**   11.–12. Words that drop **silent e**

1. _____   2. _____
3. _____   4. _____
5. _____   6. _____
7. _____   8. _____
9. _____   10. _____
11. _____   12. _____

Write Content Words to complete the exercises.

13. The f_____ of one's body during the track-and-field events of pole vault and high jump is crucial to success.

14. The pole vaulter e_____ herself over the crossbar by using a pole made of f_____.

15. A soft pit c_____ the athlete's landing during the high-jump event.

16. Dom v_____ over the t_____ crossbar that was set upon two v_____ posts.

Content Words
- flexion
- vaulted
- vertical
- elevated
- cushioned
- fiberglass
- transverse

Vocabulary Words
- impractical
- practice
- inquisitive
- requisition

high jump

Challenge Words
_____
_____

pole vault

105

27.2 Vocabulary Suffixes

Prefix		Root		Suffix	
im-	not	pract	to do	-ical	related to
in-	into	quisit	seek	-ice	state of
re-	back			-ive	inclined to
				-ion	state of

Write the Vocabulary Words.

1. _____
2. _____
3. _____
4. _____

Refer to the table to complete the exercises. Write the word that is being defined.

5. related to doing something that is not useful _____
6. inclined to seek out knowledge; curious _____
7. a state of seeking or requesting something that is required _____
8. the state of doing something repeatedly so as to become proficient or to improve _____

Write Vocabulary Words to complete the sentences.

9. Tyler will _____ his vaulting technique numerous times before perfecting his style.
10. During a meeting with an Olympic pole vaulter, Maya was very _____ and asked an abundance of questions.
11. Coach Williams put in a _____ for new pit cushions and vaulting poles.
12. Since high-jump shoes include spikes for increased traction, regular track shoes can be _____ for high jumpers to use.
13. A high-jump technique, called the straddle, seemed to be _____, so athletes tried to alter their jumping techniques.
14. Dick Fosbury began to _____ a new technique of leaping sideways across the transverse crossbar, and he successfully revolutionized the high-jump event with his new technique called the Fosbury Flop.

Pattern Words
dosage
storage
percentage
availability
impossibility
responsibility
statistically
immediately
scholarship
sportsmanship
achievement
arrangement

Content Words
flexion
vaulted
vertical
elevated
cushioned
fiberglass
transverse

Vocabulary Words
impractical
practice
inquisitive
requisition

Name _____

27.3
Word Study Strategies
Suffixes

A suffix is an affix. Affixes expand the meaning or function of a word.

Suffixes
-age = place of, state of
-ly = characteristic of, forms an adverb from an adjective
-ility = forms a noun
-ment = state of, process of
-ship = state of, quality of

Pattern Words
dosage
storage
percentage
availability
impossibility
responsibility
statistically
immediately
scholarship
sportsmanship
achievement
arrangement

Write the Pattern Word that matches each definition.

1. reliability _____
2. a place of safekeeping _____
3. a state of awarding money _____
4. a quality of fair conduct _____
5. a state of accomplishment _____
6. a state of placement or order _____
7. a state of proportion within a group _____
8. something not capable of happening _____
9. having the characteristic of informative pieces _____

Content Words
flexion
vaulted
vertical
elevated
cushioned
fiberglass
transverse

Add or subtract letters to write list words.

10. available − le + ility = _____
11. vertically − ly = _____
12. dose − e + age = _____
13. immediate + ly = _____
14. percent + age = _____
15. inquisitively − ly = _____
16. scholar + ship = _____

Vocabulary Words
impractical
practice
inquisitive
requisition

Write each list word from the pronunciation shown.

17. /ˈflek shən/ _____
18. /im ˈprak ti kəl/ _____
19. /re kwə ˈzi shən/ _____
20. /ˈkoo shənd/ _____
21. /tranz ˈvûrs/ _____

© Spelling Plus Grade 6

A graphic organizer is a drawing that shows how words or ideas fit together. A flow chart is a graphic organizer that shows the flow or process of a particular activity. Complete the graphic organizer with list words.

27.4
Writing Suffixes

The Sport of Pole Vaulting

1. First, the pole vaulter grasps a long pole and runs toward a horizontal, _____ crossbar that is set between two upright, _____ posts. The crossbar is _____ high above the ground.

2. The pole vaulter has the _____ to clear the crossbar with his or her body and should consistently _____.

3. Next, at the end of the short runway, the pole vaulter digs the pole's tip into the vault box in the ground. The vault box is essential in the _____ of a successful pole vault.

4. Then, the pole vaulter _____ swings his or her body upward feetfirst toward the crossbar. As the feet reach the crossbar, the vaulter does a handstand to thrust the body feetfirst across and over the crossbar. These actions require _____ from both the athlete's body and the pole which is made of bendable _____.

5. While at the top of the crossbar, the pole vaulter turns facedown and releases his or her grip on the pole.

6. Finally, the pole vaulter drops toward a thick, _____ pad. The location and _____ of the pad is vital for the safe landing of the vaulter.

Pattern Words
dosage
storage
percentage
availability
impossibility
responsibility
statistically
immediately
scholarship
sportsmanship
achievement
arrangement

Content Words
flexion
vaulted
vertical
elevated
cushioned
fiberglass
transverse

Vocabulary Words
impractical
practice
inquisitive
requisition

7. On a separate piece of paper, write an informative process essay about a particular sport in which you have participated. Use a graphic organizer to plan your informative essay. Use several list words and proofread your work.

Name _____

28.2
Word Analysis
Suffixes

Pattern Words

dietary
imaginary
nervous
continuous
courageous
heroism
journalism
acceptable
incomparable
insurmountable
incorruptible
inexhaustible

A suffix is a word part that is added to the ending of a root or a root with a prefix.

Write Pattern Words to complete the exercises. Sort the words according to their spelling when adding the suffix. The suffixes are -able, -ary, -ible, -ism, and -ous.

1.–8. Words that do not change

1. _____
3. _____
5. _____
7. _____
9. _____
11. _____

9.–12. Words that drop **silent e**

2. _____
4. _____
6. _____
8. _____
10. _____
12. _____

Write Content Words to complete the exercises.

13. The shot put, javelin, and discus are throwing events in track-and-field competitions that consist of h_____ objects over an e_____.

14. In throwing events, the winner is determined by a l_____ m_____ of the length of the longest throw.

15. The shot used in the shot put is a heavy metal ball. The women's shot is 4 kilograms and the men's shot weighs 7.26 k_____.

16. To throw the discus or to put the shot, the athlete generates c_____ force by spinning his or her body before throwing.

17. Throwing events are held in the midfield area of the s_____.

Content Words

linear
hurling
stadium
expanse
kilograms
centrifugal
measurement

Vocabulary Words

projectile
subjection
impulse
propulsion

Challenge Words

_____
_____

shot put
discus
javelin

© Spelling Plus Grade 6
109

28.2 Vocabulary Suffixes

Prefix		Root		Suffix	
pro-	forward	ject	throw	-ile	related to
sub-	under	puls	drive	-ion	state of
im-	in				

Write the Vocabulary Words.

1. _____
2. _____
3. _____
4. _____

Refer to the table to complete the exercises. Match each word to its definition.

_____ 5. subjection   a. the state of bringing under control

_____ 6. projectile   b. the state of driving something forward by force

_____ 7. impulse   c. an object that is thrown forward

_____ 8. propulsion   d. a sudden drive to act

Write Vocabulary Words to complete the sentences.

9. Sonia researched the history of the javelin throw in the Olympics. She learned that a javelin is a _____ since it is thrown forward.

10. Participants in the javelin throw provide the driving force, or _____, by first running several meters to gain momentum and then throwing the javelin.

11. Sonia learned that the weight and length of a javelin are in _____ to federation rules.

12. While researching the javelin throw, Sonia had a sudden _____ to try throwing a javelin.

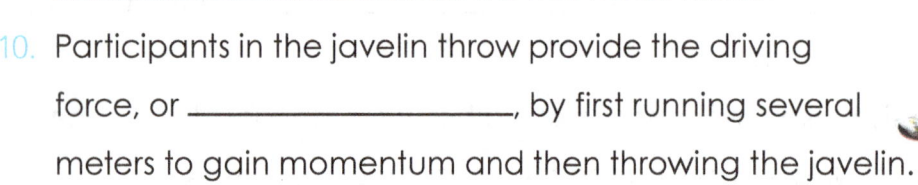

Choose the best meaning for each underlined word.

13. Sonia found throwing the javelin to be an <u>insurmountable</u> task.
    - ○ not able to be understood
    - ○ not able to be overcome

14. She decided to pursue a career in <u>journalism</u>.
    - ○ the act of writing journals or periodicals
    - ○ the act of writing poems

Pattern Words
dietary
imaginary
nervous
continuous
courageous
heroism
journalism
acceptable
incomparable
insurmountable
incorruptible
inexhaustible

Content Words
linear
hurling
stadium
expanse
kilograms
centrifugal
measurement

Vocabulary Words
projectile
subjection
impulse
propulsion

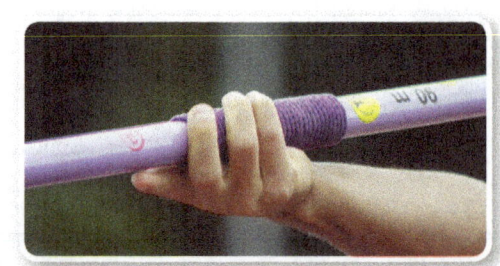

Name _____

28.3
Word Study Strategies
Suffixes

A suffix is an affix. Affixes expand the meaning or function of a word.

Suffixes
-able = is able
-ible = is able
-ous = quality of
-ary = of, related to
-ism = act of, state of

Write the Pattern Word that matches each definition.

1. not able to be compared _____
2. able to be accepted _____
3. having the quality of continuing _____
4. related to the imagination _____
5. the act of being a hero _____
6. not able to be exhausted _____
7. having the quality of courage _____
8. not able to be overcome _____
9. related to diet _____

Use the meaning of each related form to write a list word.

10. **Corrupt** is ruined.
    Corruptible is able to be ruined.
    _____ is not able to be ruined.

11. **Central** describes the center.
    A **fugitive** is one who runs away.
    _____ force is a force directed away from a center.

12. To **compare** is to view in relationship to something else.
    Comparable is similar or capable of comparison.
    _____ is not able to be compared.

13. A **span** is a distance.
    Expand is to spread out.
    An _____ is something spread out over an extensive distance.

Pattern Words
dietary
imaginary
nervous
continuous
courageous
heroism
journalism
acceptable
incomparable
insurmountable
incorruptible
inexhaustible

Content Words
linear
hurling
stadium
expanse
kilograms
centrifugal
measurement

Vocabulary Words
projectile
subjection
impulse
propulsion

Let the words of my mouth and the meditation of my heart be acceptable in Your sight, O LORD, my strength and my Redeemer. Psalm 19:14

Danielle made note cards to prepare for an informative oral report on three track-and-field events. Read her note cards. Write the missing words.

28.4
Writing Suffixes

The shot put is one of the competitions in track-and-field sports. In the shot put, an athlete pushes or puts a heavy metal ball, called a shot, for the greatest distance possible. As in other throwing events, winning is determined by a __1__ of the longest throw.

To gain momentum in the shot put, an athlete positions the shot against the side of his or her neck between the shoulder and the jawbone, spins quickly to gain __2__ force, and then extends his or her arm, releasing the shot.

In the javelin throw, athletes throw a javelin, which is a type of spear. Throwers begin each throw by running four meters before quickly leaning back to throw the javelin. The javelin must be thrown overhand; no other arm movement is __3__.

Although the javelin looks like a dangerous __4__, there is no need to feel __5__ about the javelin throw. The javelin is never thrown at a target, and the point of the javelin must hit the ground first for the throw to count.

Another hurling event is the discus throw. A discus is a flat, disk-shaped metal plate that is thrown for distance. The women's discus weighs one kilogram and the men's discus weighs two __6__. Centrifugal force provides the __7__ for the discus.

As with all track-and-field events, throwing the discus requires a __8__ series of training sessions. Many Olympic champions have practiced throwing the discus for years before winning a medal. Success in throwing is not gained on an __9__.

Pattern Words
dietary
imaginary
nervous
continuous
courageous
heroism
journalism
acceptable
incomparable
insurmountable
incorruptible
inexhaustible

Content Words
linear
hurling
stadium
expanse
kilograms
centrifugal
measurement

Vocabulary Words
projectile
subjection
impulse
propulsion

1. _____   2. _____   3. _____
4. _____   5. _____   6. _____
7. _____   8. _____   9. _____

Name _____

29.2
Word Analysis
R-Controlled Vowels

Pattern Words

angular
revered
souvenir
departed
nourished
downpour
formidable
domineering
unnecessary
disheartened
administrator
entertainment

R-controlled vowels are vowels or combinations of vowels that precede *r*. The letter *r* affects the sound of the vowel or vowels. The /âr/ sound is heard in **unnecessary**. The /är/ sound is heard in **departed**. The /îr/ sound is heard in **revered**. The /ôr/ sound is heard in **downpour**. The /ûr/ sound is heard in **angular**.

Write Pattern Words to complete the exercises. Sort the r-controlled vowel words and circle each r-controlled spelling.

1. /âr/ spelled **ar**
2.–3. /ôr/ spelled **or**, **our**
4.–5. /är/ spelled **ar**, **ear**
6.–8. /îr/ spelled **eer**, **ere**, **ir**
9.–12. /ûr/ spelled **ar**, **er**, **or**, **our**

1. _____ 2. _____
3. _____ 4. _____
5. _____ 6. _____
7. _____ 8. _____
9. _____ 10. _____
11. _____ 12. _____

Write Content Words to complete the exercises.

13. The long jump is a track-and-field contest that measures an athlete's ability to jump a h_____ distance. The e_____ of competitors occurs after each athlete performs three jumps.

14. C_____ in the long jump have strong abdominal and leg muscles and are t_____ athletes.

15. The official f_____ on his job. He measured the p_____ distance of each i_____ in the sand after each long jump.

Content Words

precise
focused
horizontal
elimination
indentation
contestants
tremendous

Vocabulary Words

concerned
discernment
introspective
retrospect

Challenge Words

_____
_____

long jump

113

29.2 Vocabulary — R-Controlled Vowels

Prefix		Root		Suffix	
con-	thoroughly	cern	make certain, distinguished	-ed	makes verbs past tense
dis-	apart	spect	examine	-ment	that which
intro-	inside			-ive	inclined to
retro-	backward				

Pattern Words
angular
revered
souvenir
departed
nourished
downpour
formidable
domineering
unnecessary
disheartened
administrator
entertainment

Content Words
precise
focused
horizontal
elimination
indentation
contestants
tremendous

Vocabulary Words
concerned
discernment
introspective
retrospect

Write the Vocabulary Words.

1. _____ 2. _____
3. _____ 4. _____

Refer to the table to complete the exercises. Write the word that is being defined.

5. inclined to examining one's own feelings; thoughtful _____
6. that which shows distinguished judgment, perception, or sensitivity _____
7. to look back and examine or remember events; a recollection _____
8. to be thoroughly anxious about a certain situation; worried _____

Write Vocabulary Words to complete the sentences.

9. Gerald was _____ about securing one of the eight spots in the long-jump finals.
10. Brandi was _____ as she reviewed the new competition rules.
11. A long-jump athlete should use _____ when approaching the takeoff board during the run to the sandpit.
12. In _____, Clint believed that he could improve his distances from the long-jump meet, so he resolved to practice diligently before the next competition.

Choose the word that matches each definition.

13. needless
    ○ downpour   ○ departed   ○ unnecessary
14. admired
    ○ angular   ○ horizontal ○ revered

Name _____

29.3

Word Study Strategies
R-Controlled Vowels

Use the Spelling Dictionary to answer each question.
1. What is the pronunciation for **revered**? _____
2. What is the part of speech for **formidable**? _____
3. What is the definition for **horizontal**? _____
_____
4. What is the sample sentence for **horizontal**? _____
_____
5. What is the pronunciation for **angular**? _____
6. What is the part of speech for **downpour**? _____
7. What is the definition for **indentation**? _____
8. What is the sample sentence for **concerned**? _____
_____

Pattern Words
angular
revered
souvenir
departed
nourished
downpour
formidable
domineering
unnecessary
disheartened
administrator
entertainment

An inference is a conclusion reached by looking at facts. Look at the facts given in each sentence to infer the missing list word. Write the list word.

9. Tabitha and Rhea diligently practiced their sheet music and marching drills for three weeks. The girls were part of the opening ceremony _____ for a track-and-field meet.

10. Mrs. Ruthe was asked to lead and supervise all field activities during the meet. She served as the _____ for the event.

11. As a long-jump official, Dale wanted to do his job well by measuring exact distances. His measurements were very _____.

12. Several athletes were sad and discouraged about their distances in the long jump. They were very _____.

13. Coach Walter counseled a particular athlete who had a bossy demeanor after the meet. He was asked to pray about and work on his _____ attitude.

14. Charlotte ran to the front of the stadium, but the bus was not there. Unfortunately, the bus had already _____.

Content Words
precise
focused
horizontal
elimination
indentation
contestants
tremendous

Vocabulary Words
concerned
discernment
introspective
retrospect

But the fruit of the Spirit is love, joy, peace, longsuffering, kindness, goodness, faithfulness, gentleness, self-control.
Galatians 5:22–23

Chelsea is a student at Calvary Middle School. She interviewed Yuriko, a student athlete who competes in the track-and-field event of the long jump. Read the dialogue. Write the list word that matches each underlined pronunciation.

29.4

Writing R-Controlled Vowels

An Interview with a Long Jumper

CHELSEA: Yuriko, how did you become interested in the long jump, and how long have you been a participant?

YURIKO: I cannot give you a /pri 'sīs/ time when I first became interested in the long jump, but in /'re trə spekt/, I believe I have been jumping in track meets for two and a half years.

CHELSEA: Do you recall your most challenging meet?

YURIKO: Oh, yes. In a meet held last spring, the condition of the runway track /kən 'sûrnd/ me because of a recent /'doun pôr/. Everything was still wet, so avoiding a slip on my takeoff would be a /fôr 'mi də bəl/ task.

CHELSEA: Were you able to make a good jump?

YURIKO: Not on my first attempt, but I refused to feel /dis 'här tənd/. I /'fō kəsd/ on making my next jump count, took off at top speed, and made a /tri 'men dəs/ leap into the sandpit.

CHELSEA: How did you do?

YURIKO: I made the longest jump of all the /kən 'tes tənts/ and avoided /i li mə 'nā shən/. The wet sand was actually beneficial because the /in den 'tā shən/ of my jump was easy to see and measure. I won first place that day!

Pattern Words
angular
revered
souvenir
departed
nourished
downpour
formidable
domineering
unnecessary
disheartened
administrator
entertainment

Content Words
precise
focused
horizontal
elimination
indentation
contestants
tremendous

Vocabulary Words
concerned
discernment
introspective
retrospect

1. _____
2. _____
3. _____
4. _____
5. _____
6. _____
7. _____
8. _____
9. _____
10. _____
11. _____

Name _____

30.1

Review Chapters 25–29
Chapter 25

Pattern Words

Chapter 25 Prefixes	Chapter 26 Prefixes	Chapter 27 Suffixes	Chapter 28 Suffixes	Chapter 29 R-Controlled Vowels
antistress	mistreated	dosage	dietary	angular
antibiotics	mismanaged	storage	imaginary	revered
disability	multicultural	percentage	nervous	souvenir
dislocation	multitalented	availability	continuous	departed
embodied	postexercise	impossibility	courageous	nourished
embraced	postoperative	responsibility	heroism	downpour
immovable	proactive	statistically	journalism	formidable
improvement	prolonged	immediately	acceptable	domineering
invariably	superathlete	scholarship	incomparable	unnecessary
incredulous	supereffective	sportsmanship	insurmountable	disheartened
midsole	underestimate	achievement	incorruptible	administrator
midfield	undernourished	arrangement	inexhaustible	entertainment

Content Words

sprinter	fatigue	flexion	linear	precise
elongate	stamina	vaulted	hurling	focused
multilane	disciplined	vertical	stadium	horizontal
crouching	surpassed	elevated	expanse	elimination
champions	conditioning	cushioned	kilograms	indentation
simultaneously	strategizing	fiberglass	centrifugal	contestants
counterclockwise	dehydration	transverse	measurement	tremendous

Vocabulary Words

abruptly	duration	impractical	projectile	concerned
disruption	enduring	practice	subjection	discernment
revived	opposed	inquisitive	impulse	introspective
vivacious	supposing	requisition	propulsion	retrospect

Read Chapter 25 Pattern Words. Follow the directions given.

1. Circle the Pattern Words that contain the prefix **em-**.
2. Box the Pattern Words that contain the prefix **mid-**.
3. Make a dot next to the Pattern Words that contain the prefix **anti-**.
4. Place a star next to the Pattern Words that contain the prefix **in-**.
5. Write a check mark next to the Pattern Words that contain the prefix **dis-**.
6. Underline the Pattern Words that contain the prefix **im-**.

© Spelling Plus Grade 6

Read each word. Decide if it is spelled correctly or incorrectly. Fill in the circle. Write each word correctly.

30.2

Review Chapters 25–29
Chapters 26–27

	Correct	Incorrect	
1. postopirative	○	○	_____
2. supereffective	○	○	_____
3. misstreated	○	○	_____
4. multiculturall	○	○	_____
5. prolonged	○	○	_____
6. mismannaged	○	○	_____
7. undernurished	○	○	_____
8. postexercise	○	○	_____
9. proactive	○	○	_____

mistreated
mismanaged
multicultural
multitalented
postexercise
postoperative
proactive
prolonged
superathlete
supereffective
underestimate
undernourished

Find the words in the word search. Circle them and write them on the lines. The words go across, down, and backwards. Some of the words share letters. Complete the sentence below by writing the remaining letters in the order that they appear.

```
i m p o s s i b i l i t y t h s
p i h s r a l o h c s e r e s t
p o n s i b i l i t y a t h l o
y t i l i b a l i a v a e t e r
s t o s i m m e d i a t e l y a
y l l a c i t s i t a t s p o g
a c h i e v e m e n t r s m e
t n e m e g n a r r a a n s h i
p e r c e n t a g e g a s o d p
```

dosage
storage
percentage
availability
impossibility
responsibility
statistically
immediately
scholarship
sportsmanship
achievement
arrangement

_____ _____ _____
_____ _____ _____
_____ _____ _____
_____

It is __ __ __ __ __ __ __ __ __ __ __ __ __ __ __ __ __ __
of __ __ __ __ __ __ __ __ __ __ __ __ __ show good
__ __ __ __ __ __ __ __ __ __ __ __ __.

Name _____

30.3

Review Chapters 25–29
Chapters 28–29

Write each word that is being defined.

1. unlike anything else ___ ___ ___ ___ ☐ ___ ___ ___ ___ ___ ___
2. related to the imagination ___ ___ ___ ☐ ___ ___ ___ ___ ___
3. jumpy ___ ___ ☐ ___ ___ ___
4. tireless ___ ___ ___ ___ ☐ ___ ___ ___ ___ ___
5. able to be accepted ___ ___ ___ ___ ___ ___ ___ ☐ ___
6. related to diet ___ ___ ___ ___ ☐ ___ ___
7. unconquerable ___ ___ ___ ☐ ___ ___ ___ ___ ___ ___ ___ ___ ___
8. not able to be ruined ___ ___ ___ ___ ___ ___ ☐ ___ ___ ___ ___ ___
9. the act of being a hero ___ ___ ___ ☐ ___ ___ ___
10. having the quality of courage ___ ___ ___ ☐ ___ ___ ___ ___ ___
11. having the quality of continuing ___ ___ ___ ☐ ___ ___ ___ ___ ___ ___ ☐

Word list:
- dietary
- imaginary
- nervous
- continuous
- courageous
- heroism
- journalism
- acceptable
- incomparable
- insurmountable
- incorruptible
- inexhaustible

Write the boxed letters above in the order that they appear to complete the sentence.

12. During the lecture about journalism, the speaker explained that disabled athletes who participate in the Paralympics are called ___ ___ ___ ___ ___ ___ ___ ___ ___ ___.

Circle the correct r-controlled vowel spelling that completes each word. Write each word correctly.

Word bank:
- angular
- revered
- souvenir
- departed
- nourished
- downpour
- formidable
- domineering
- unnecessary
- disheartened
- administrator
- entertainment

#	Word	Option 1	Option 2	Answer
13.	downp ___	our	or	_____
14.	domin ___ ing	ere	eer	_____
15.	rev ___ d	ir	ere	_____
16.	unnecess ___ y	ar	are	_____
17.	ent ___ tainment	our	er	_____
18.	angul ___	ar	er	_____
19.	f ___ midable	our	or	_____
20.	dep ___ ted	ear	ar	_____
21.	souven ___	eer	ir	_____
22.	dish ___ tened	ear	ar	_____
23.	administrat ___	our	or	_____
24.	n ___ rished	er	our	_____

Spelling Plus Grade 6 — 119

Read the paragraph. Write a Content Word in each shape box.

30.4

Review Chapters 25–29
Content and Vocabulary Words

Track-and-Field Sports

Track-and-field sports include short- and long-distance running, jumping, and throwing events. A ▢▢▢▢▢▢▢▢ runs a short distance on a ▢▢▢▢▢▢▢▢ track. Long-distance runners battle ▢▢▢▢▢▢▢ and ▢▢▢▢▢▢▢▢▢▢▢. Pole vaulters and high jumpers take a ▢▢▢▢▢▢▢▢ leap over a crossbar. Vaulters and jumpers land on a ▢▢▢▢▢▢▢▢ surface. Throwing events and the long-jump competition are won by contestants with the greatest ▢▢▢▢▢▢▢▢▢▢▢▢▢▢▢ in the event. Track-and-field sports are exciting to watch.

sprinter
multilane
champions
fatigue
conditioning
dehydration
flexion
vertical
cushioned
linear
stadium
measurement
precise
elimination
contestants

	A	B	C	D	E	F	G	H
1	dis-	in-	con-	pract	ject	-ly	-ation	-ice
2	en-	ab-	pro-	quisit	dur	-ical	-ing	-tion
3	re-	intro-	sub-	cern	spect	-ment	-ile	-ous
4	op-	im-	rupt	puls	pos	-ive	-ed	-ion

abruptly
disruption
revived
duration
enduring
opposed
impractical
practice
inquisitive
projectile
subjection
impulse
concerned
discernment
introspective

Find the coordinates given. Write the Vocabulary Words.

1. B4 + D1 + F2 = _____
2. A2 + E2 + G2 = _____
3. C3 + E1 + H4 = _____
4. C2 + E1 + G3 = _____
5. E2 + G1 = _____
6. D1 + H1 = _____
7. A4 + E4 + G4 = _____
8. B1 + D2 + F4 = _____
9. A1 + C4 + H4 = _____
10. B3 + E3 + F4 = _____

Name _____

31.2

Word Analysis
Frequently Misspelled Words

Pattern Words
privilege
definitely
sincerely
miniature
necessary
separately
meticulous
restaurant
conscientious
embarrassed
perseverance
congratulations

Write Pattern Words to complete the exercises. Sort the frequently misspelled words according to their pronunciation.

1. /'pri və lij/ _____
2. /sin 'sîr lē/ _____
3. /im 'bâr əsd/ _____
4. /kont shē 'ent shəs/ _____
5. /'ne sə sâr ē/ _____
6. /pûr sə 'vîr ənts/ _____
7. /'res tə ränt/ _____
8. /kən gra chə 'lā shənz/ _____
9. /'de fə nit lē/ _____
10. /mə 'ti kyə ləs/ _____
11. /'mi nē ə choor/ _____
12. /'se pə rət lē/ _____

Content Words
divot
torque
titanium
hazards
accuracy
trajectory
maintenance

Write Content Words to complete the exercises.

13. The sport of golf requires a_____ in swinging clubs to advance a small, hard ball over a course of play.
14. Many popular golf clubs are made of a strong, lightweight metal called t_____. The angle of a golf club and the t_____ of its shaft are necessary for a good path, or t_____, of the golf ball.
15. The m_____ of water h_____ and each d_____ that is dug out of the green is an industrious job.

Vocabulary Words
dignify
dignity
sociable
society

Challenge Words
_____
_____

golf

© Spelling Plus Grade 6   121

Prefix	Root		Suffix	
	dign	worthy	-ify	to make
	soci	companion	-ity	state of
			-able	is able
			-ety	state of

31.2
Vocabulary
Frequently Misspelled Words

Pattern Words
privilege
definitely
sincerely
miniature
necessary
separately
meticulous
restaurant
conscientious
embarrassed
perseverance
congratulations

Content Words
divot
torque
titanium
hazards
accuracy
trajectory
maintenance

Vocabulary Words
dignify
dignity
sociable
society

Write the Vocabulary Words.

1. _____
2. _____
3. _____
4. _____

Refer to the table to complete the exercises. Write the word that is being defined.

5. a state of being worthy; self-respect _____
6. to make worthy of; to honor, distinguish, or give distinction _____
7. able to seek out the company of other people or engage in social interaction; friendly; outgoing _____
8. a state of companionship; a group of people, generally with a common interest or role _____

Write Vocabulary Words to complete the sentences.

9. Arthur joined a golf club that was a big part of the local _____.
10. Arthur and Franco were _____ with the newest members of the golf association.
11. Arthur and Franco kept their _____ during the long tournament and did not cheat while keeping record of their score.
12. Arthur chose to _____ the various sponsors of the golf tournament by acknowledging each one during his closing speech.

Choose the word that matches each definition.

13. conscientious; thorough; careful
    - divot
    - meticulous
    - privilege
14. persistence; determination
    - sincerely
    - perseverance
    - torque

Name _____

31.3

Word Study Strategies
Frequently Misspelled Words

Idioms are fun ways to talk about everyday things. Write the list word that is suggested by each idiom in the sentences.

1. When someone gives you a pat on the back, he or she is offering you their _____.
2. If you turn beet red, then you are _____.
3. If you always hang in there, then you have _____.
4. If someone is a social butterfly, then he or she is a very _____ person.
5. When someone goes through something with a fine-tooth comb, he or she is very _____.
6. If you eat at a mom-and-pop establishment, then you are eating at a quaint, little _____.
7. If someone dots i's and crosses t's, then he or she is _____.

Number each word in alphabetical order. Write the words in the order numbered.

___ privilege   ___ definitely   ___ sincerely   ___ miniature
___ necessary   ___ separately   ___ restaurant   ___ torque
___ trajectory   ___ maintenance   ___ dignity   ___ society

8. _____
9. _____
10. _____
11. _____
12. _____
13. _____
14. _____
15. _____
16. _____
17. _____
18. _____
19. _____

Pattern Words
privilege
definitely
sincerely
miniature
necessary
separately
meticulous
restaurant
conscientious
embarrassed
perseverance
congratulations

Content Words
divot
torque
titanium
hazards
accuracy
trajectory
maintenance

Vocabulary Words
dignify
dignity
sociable
society

© Spelling Plus Grade 6

123

Eliana wrote a blog about a fund-raising golf tournament. A blog is an online personal journal with individual comments and reflections. Read Eliana's blog and revise the text before the online post. Use proofreading marks. Correctly write the misspelled words.

31.4
Writing
Frequently Misspelled Words

Eliana's Blog

I am exhausted from a long day on the golf course, but there is much to reflect on. today's tournament was held as a socaible, fund-raising event to find a cure for leukemia. I had the privelege of spending the day. With many children who suffer from this disease

    The day started off with a breakfast buffet in the club restuarant where I met Isabella, a ten-year-old girl who has leukemia. isabella was happy and full of life, and we became instant friends. She told me that she was looking forward to seeing the governor and mayor play against each other in the nine-hole golf tournament. Not long after Isabella mentioned them, Governor Broberg and Mayor Wood each arrived seperately to the event.

    Before we knew it, the tournament was underway. spectators followed the game from one hole to the next. Both players played with acuracy and stayed under par until eighth hole. Then things started to fall apart. For the governor. He kept hitting the golf ball into hazerds—a sand bunker and a little Stream! It seemed that he was going to lose, but he stayed focused. On the ninth hole, he swung his golf club, and the tragectory of the ball determined its path straight down the fairway. Cheers erupted after the ball hit the cup. Plunk! A hole in one! Mayor Wood offered Governor Broberg his congradulations.

    I believe it it is neccessary to draw more attention to finding a Cure for leukemia. Isabella's spirit of perserverance sincirely touched my heart. She is a hero to me I am definitly glad that I attended this event. What can you do to help

> We also glory in tribulations, knowing that tribulation produces perseverance; and perseverance, character; and character, hope. Romans 5:3–4

Proofreading Marks
- ○ Circle misspellings.
- ≡ Make a capital letter.
- ⊙ Add a period.
- ℓ Delete.
- ∧ Add something.
- / Make a small letter.
- ¶ Make a new paragraph.

Pattern Words
privilege
definitely
sincerely
miniature
necessary
separately
meticulous
restaurant
conscientious
embarrassed
perseverance
congratulations

Content Words
divot
torque
titanium
hazards
accuracy
trajectory
maintenance

Vocabulary Words
dignify
dignity
sociable
society

1. _____
2. _____
3. _____
4. _____
5. _____
6. _____
7. _____
8. _____
9. _____
10. _____
11. _____
12. _____

Name _____

32.2
Word Analysis
Words from French and Italian

Pattern Words
- ballet
- bouquet
- gourmet
- etiquette
- chauffeur
- chandelier
- finale
- adagio
- rotunda
- parapet
- spaghetti
- macaroni

Content Words
- poised
- exhibition
- dressage
- obstacles
- equestrian
- prestigious
- domesticated

Vocabulary Words
- auction
- auctioneer
- circumspectly
- circumvent

Many words in the English language originally came from the French and Italian languages. Knowledge of word origins helps in building spelling and vocabulary skills.

The first six Pattern Words are derived from French. The last six Pattern Words are derived from Italian.

Write Pattern Words to complete the exercises. Sort the words by derivation.

1.–6. Words from Italian   7.–12. Words from French

1. _____   2. _____
3. _____   4. _____
5. _____   6. _____
7. _____   8. _____
9. _____   10. _____
11. _____   12. _____

Write Content Words to complete the exercises.

13. Sports relevant to horsemanship are known as e_____ sports.

14. Horses have been d_____ for centuries.

15. Training in d_____ involves working closely with a horse to perfect its gait in walking, trotting, and cantering.

16. One p_____ event in equestrian circles is an e_____ of the graceful and p_____ Lipizzaner stallions.

17. Rodeo competitions test a horse's agility in avoiding o_____ in events such as barrel racing.

Challenge Words
_____
_____

horseback riding

32.2
Vocabulary Words from French and Italian

Prefix	Root		Suffix	
	auct	lasting	-ion	state of
	circum	put	-eer	one who
	spect	examine	-ly	forms an adverb
	vent	come		from an adjective

Write the Vocabulary Words.

1. _____
2. _____
3. _____
4. _____

Refer to the table to complete the exercises. Match each word to its definition.

_____ 5. auctioneer — a. to manage to go around; to avoid
_____ 6. circumvent — b. carefully examining each possibility; prudently
_____ 7. auction — c. one who asks for an increase in bidding
_____ 8. circumspectly — d. a sale using bids to increase the price of each item

Write Vocabulary Words to complete the sentences.

9. Jean-Paul went to an _____ of thoroughbred horses.
10. Because he would be buying his first horse, Jean-Paul studied the auction brochure and _____ reviewed the qualities of each horse being sold.
11. Jean-Paul waited for the _____ to announce bidding on a beautiful Arabian stallion.
12. Studying the history and temperament of horses would help Jean-Paul _____ problems with his horse's training.

Choose the best meaning for each underlined word.

13. Pierre cantered his horse near the castle to view the <u>parapet</u>.
    ○ a low wall or railing used as protection
    ○ a hanging lighting fixture
14. Jacques dismounted his horse and entered the <u>rotunda</u>.
    ○ a lavish ballroom
    ○ a round building often covered by a dome

Pattern Words
ballet
bouquet
gourmet
etiquette
chauffeur
chandelier
finale
adagio
rotunda
parapet
spaghetti
macaroni

Content Words
poised
exhibition
dressage
obstacles
equestrian
prestigious
domesticated

Vocabulary Words
auction
auctioneer
circumspectly
circumvent

Name _____

32.3

Word Study Strategies
Words from French and Italian

A <mark>subordinating conjunction</mark> is a conjunction that joins two clauses, an independent clause and a dependent clause, into one sentence. An independent clause can stand alone because it contains both a subject and a predicate and expresses a complete thought. A dependent clause may contain both a subject and a predicate, but does not express a complete thought. A dependent clause may begin with a subordinating conjunction. Some subordinating conjunctions are *after, although, as, because, since, when, where,* and *while.*

Complete each sentence by adding an independent clause. Underline the subordinating conjunction. Notice that a comma is used in sentences that begin with dependent clauses.

1. After Sofia watched the equestrian event, _____
   _____

2. Although it was not the finale, _____

3. Because Antonio won the race, _____

4. When equestrian events are televised, _____
   _____

5. While the chauffeur waited, _____

A <mark>complex sentence</mark> is a combination of an independent and a dependent clause. A dependent clause often begins with a subordinating conjunction.

Read each complex sentence. Write the independent clause on the first line. Write the dependent clause on the second line. The first one is done for you.

6. Lucia entered an exhibition of dressage since her horse was well trained.
   Lucia entered an exibition of dressage
   _____
   since her horse was well trained

7. As the piano played an adagio, the horses paraded around the ring.
   _____
   _____

8. The horse show was held in the rotunda because it was a prestigious event.
   _____
   _____

9. When she saw the Lipizzaner horses perform, Liza thought of ballet.
   _____
   _____

Pattern Words
ballet
bouquet
gourmet
etiquette
chauffeur
chandelier
finale
adagio
rotunda
parapet
spaghetti
macaroni

Content Words
poised
exhibition
dressage
obstacles
equestrian
prestigious
domesticated

Vocabulary Words
auction
auctioneer
circumspectly
circumvent

A **quatrain** is a poem with four lines that rhyme. Sometimes a lengthy poem is written with multiple quatrains. Read the poem. Write the missing words on the lines.

32.4

Writing Words from French and Italian

At the Horse Show

From my seat, high up in the e_____ hall
I watched the horses perform for us all.
Some classical music, an a_____,
Introduced the magnificent horses below.

    As p_____ riders on horseback went through their paces,
  Looks of amazement appeared on our faces.
  The jumpers performed, leaping o_____ with ease.
  Taking jumps of all heights, just like a breeze.

In the center ring, the Lipizzaners pranced.
Their hooves left the ground, and they leapt and danced.
Like a beautiful b_____, so graceful and light.
I cannot imagine a more lovely sight.

    At last, the f_____ of the e_____ show
  Began with applause in the circle below.
  When all the horses had performed for the day,
  Each rider received a floral b_____.

Pattern Words
ballet
bouquet
gourmet
etiquette
chauffeur
chandelier
finale
adagio
rotunda
parapet
spaghetti
macaroni

Content Words
poised
exhibition
dressage
obstacles
equestrian
prestigious
domesticated

Vocabulary Words
auction
auctioneer
circumspectly
circumvent

A **cinquain** is a poem with five lines that do not rhyme. The cinquain form of poetry always follows a pattern. An example is shown on the right.

Line 1: the subject of the poem   Dressage
Line 2: two adjectives that describe the subject   Poised, prestigious
Line 3: three action verbs that relate to the subject   Walking, trotting, cantering
Line 4: a sentence about the subject   Well-trained horses compete for awards.
Line 5: a synonym of the subject   Horsemanship

On a separate piece of paper, write a quatrain or a cinquain, utilizing several list words.

Name _____

33.2
Word Analysis
Words from Spanish

Pattern Words
- fiesta
- guitar
- maize
- tortilla
- alfalfa
- pronto
- burrito
- anchovy
- mariachi
- enchilada
- quesadilla
- sombrero

Many words in the English language originally came from the Spanish language. Knowledge of word origins helps in building spelling and vocabulary skills.

Write Pattern Words to complete the exercises. Write the words in alphabetical order.

1. _____ 2. _____
3. _____ 4. _____
5. _____ 6. _____
7. _____ 8. _____
9. _____ 10. _____
11. _____ 12. _____

Write Content Words to complete the exercises.

13. All three types of fencing, foil, épée, and saber, build strength and d_____, as well as speed and agility.
14. Eight defensive t_____, known as parries, are used in fencing.
15. A f_____ is a movement used to mislead an opponent in order to attack.
16. A b_____ is won when a fencer scores five touches on his or her opponent in three minutes or fifteen touches in nine minutes.
17. In foil fencing, the t_____ is the only target area.
18. Attacks are i_____ from the on-guard position.
19. The p_____ of the on-guard position is a crouch with knees bent, the rear arm raised upward, and the sword arm extended forward.

Content Words
- feint
- bout
- torso
- tactics
- initiated
- posture
- dexterity

Vocabulary Words
- clarity
- declaration
- detection
- protected

Challenge Words

_____
_____

fencing

Spelling Plus Grade 6   129

33.2 Vocabulary: Words from Spanish

Prefix		Root		Suffix	
de-	thoroughly	clar	clear	-ity	state of
pro-	before	tect	cover	-ation	state of
				-ion	state of
				-ed	makes verbs past tense

Pattern Words
fiesta
guitar
maize
tortilla
alfalfa
pronto
burrito
anchovy
mariachi
enchilada
quesadilla
sombrero

Content Words
feint
bout
torso
tactics
initiated
posture
dexterity

Vocabulary Words
clarity
declaration
detection
protected

Write the Vocabulary Words.

1. _____
2. _____
3. _____
4. _____

Refer to the table to complete the exercises. Write the word that is being defined.

5. to have covered beforehand; shielded _____
6. the state of making your position thoroughly clear; an announcement _____
7. the state of thoroughly uncovering the facts _____
8. a state of being clear; lucidness _____

Write Vocabulary Words to complete the sentences.

9. For _____, the new judge reviewed the fencing rules.
10. Participants in all three types of fencing, foil, épée, and saber, must be _____ by a proper fencing uniform.
11. A judge can make a _____ to disqualify a fencer for misconduct.
12. The _____ of a touch, which scores a point, is verified by an electronic scoring device.

Choose the word that matches each definition.

13. trick
    ○ guitar ○ feint ○ mariachi
14. festival
    ○ maize ○ fiesta ○ sombrero
15. without delay; fast
    ○ pronto ○ alfalfa ○ anchovy

Name _____

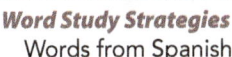

33.3

Word Study Strategies
Words from Spanish

Write a Pattern Word to fit each category.

1. party, celebration, festival, _____
2. quesadilla, burrito, enchilada, _____
3. singing, instruments, band, _____
4. burrito, enchilada, tortilla, _____
5. derby, beret, helmet, _____
6. legume, hay, plant, _____
7. fast, quickly, rapidly, _____
8. stalk, vegetable, Indian, _____
9. strings, frets, pick, _____
10. fish, fins, scales, _____

Write a list word to complete the riddles.

11. It is a trick but not a treat. _____
12. It does not have arms, although it is part of the body. _____
13. It is always safe. _____
14. It does things very well and is not clumsy. _____
15. It is an idea that has been started. _____
16. It is never bored because it is a variety of methods. _____
17. It helps with understanding in case something is confusing. _____
18. It is an announcement heard by students. _____
19. It is always helping to uncover important information. _____
20. It is a lot of exercise during a fencing match. _____
21. It is versatile and enjoys being able to change positions frequently. _____

Pattern Words
fiesta
guitar
maize
tortilla
alfalfa
pronto
burrito
anchovy
mariachi
enchilada
quesadilla
sombrero

Content Words
feint
bout
torso
tactics
initiated
posture
dexterity

Vocabulary Words
clarity
declaration
detection
protected

For the word of God is living and powerful, and sharper than any two-edged sword ... Hebrews 4:12

131

Read the journal entry about fencing. Fill in the shape boxes with Content Words to complete the journal entry.

Fencing

I have learned so much these past few weeks in my foil fencing class. Foil fencing is for beginners. The sword is lightweight, and the **torso** is the only target area. In épée fencing, the entire body is the target area, and in saber fencing, the body from the hips upward is the target area. Fencing is definitely a sport that requires more **dexterity** than I ever imagined. I am still trying to master the correct **posture** for holding the sword. I tend to hold the grip too tightly and bend my elbow out to my side instead of keeping it inward. In each **bout** that I participated in today, I kept missing my target when I **initiated** an offensive attack. When I missed, my opponent scored a point. However, I was able to use a **feint** and score a few points of my own. My coach said that he sees an improvement in my skills and **tactics**. Coach Williams also said that I could participate in the upcoming tournament. I am certainly looking forward to that!

Writing Words from Spanish

Pattern Words
fiesta
guitar
maize
tortilla
alfalfa
pronto
burrito
anchovy
mariachi
enchilada
quesadilla
sombrero

Content Words
feint
bout
torso
tactics
initiated
posture
dexterity

Vocabulary Words
clarity
declaration
detection
protected

Name _____

34.2
Word Analysis
Words from German

Pattern Words
- diesel
- seltzer
- strudel
- pretzel
- edelweiss
- liverwurst
- gesundheit
- sauerkraut
- hamburger
- frankfurter
- delicatessen
- pumpernickel

Content Words
- taut
- notch
- quiver
- tension
- graphite
- concentric
- categories

Vocabulary Words
- generation
- regenerate
- exposition
- proposition

Many words in the English language originally came from the German language. Knowledge of word origins helps in building spelling and vocabulary skills.

Write Pattern Words to complete the exercises. Sort the words by the number of syllables.

1.–4. **Two Syllables**   5.–10. **Three Syllables**
11. **Four Syllables**   12. **Five Syllables**

1. _____   2. _____
3. _____   4. _____
5. _____   6. _____
7. _____   8. _____
9. _____   10. _____
11. _____ 12. _____

Write Content Words to complete the exercises.

13. Arrows are made of aluminum or carbon g_____ and are kept in a q_____.

14. A n_____ at the end of the arrow allows the arrow to be fitted to the bowstring.

15. The string or cord on a bow must be t_____ so that when t_____ is applied, the arrow is propelled forward.

16. Archers shoot arrows at a target that usually consists of a bull's-eye and a series of c_____ circles.

17. Target, field, and flight shooting are c_____ in archery competitions.

Challenge Words
_____
_____

archery

34.2 Vocabulary — Words from German

Prefix		Root		Suffix	
re-	again	gen	birth	-er	that which, action
ex-	out of	posit	place	-ation	state of
pro-	for			-ate	to make
				-ion	state of

Pattern Words
diesel
seltzer
strudel
pretzel
edelweiss
liverwurst
gesundheit
sauerkraut
hamburger
frankfurter
delicatessen
pumpernickel

Content Words
taut
notch
quiver
tension
graphite
concentric
categories

Vocabulary Words
generation
regenerate
exposition
proposition

Write the Vocabulary Words.

1. _____
2. _____
3. _____
4. _____

Refer to the table to complete the exercises. Match each word to its definition.

_____ 5. exposition   a. to make or produce again

_____ 6. generation   b. the state of time between the birth of parents and their offspring

_____ 7. regenerate   c. the state of something being placed or offered for consideration; proposal

_____ 8. proposition   d. the state of placing items out in the view of the public; a fair or exhibition

Write Vocabulary Words to complete the sentences.

9. The archery coach offered Terrell and the team a _____ to perform at the Kern County Fair.

10. The _____ will be at the fairground in two weeks.

11. Because they had been on vacation, the team will practice daily in order to _____ their championship archery skills.

12. Terrell's parents were also archery champions, making Terrell an archer for the second _____.

Choose the best meaning for each word.

13. pumpernickel
    - ○ a dark sourdough bread
    - ○ a glazed donut
    - ○ a long twisted pastry

14. edelweiss
    - ○ a pastry
    - ○ a flower
    - ○ an animal

134

Name _____

34.3

Word Study Strategies
Words from German

Use the Spelling Dictionary to answer each question.
1. What is the pronunciation for **seltzer**? _____
2. What is the part of speech for **gesundheit**? _____
3. What is the definition for **quiver**? _____
_____
4. What is the sample sentence for **exposition**? _____
_____
5. What is the pronunciation for **exposition**? _____
6. What is the part of speech for **delicatessen**? _____
7. What is the definition for **graphite**? _____
_____
8. What is the sample sentence for **taut**? _____
_____

Look up each bold word in the Spelling Dictionary. Read each definition and write the list word that fits each category.

liverwurst, hamburger, frankfurter
9. sausage, cooked, casing, _____
10. sandwich, round, beef, _____
11. spreadable, sausage, liver, _____

diesel, generation, pretzel
12. salty, knot, crisp, _____
13. car, truck, engine, _____
14. birth, children, parents, _____

gesundheit, sauerkraut, concentric
15. sneeze, polite, comment, _____
16. circular, center, midpoint, _____
17. salt, cabbage, fermented, _____

Pattern Words
diesel
seltzer
strudel
pretzel
edelweiss
liverwurst
gesundheit
sauerkraut
hamburger
frankfurter
delicatessen
pumpernickel

Content Words
taut
notch
quiver
tension
graphite
concentric
categories

Vocabulary Words
generation
regenerate
exposition
proposition

Phillip wrote a descriptive, friendly letter to his parents. Read the letter. Write the list words that could replace the bold word or words in each sentence. Use the Spelling Dictionary.

34.4

Writing
Words from German

Dear Mom and Dad,

  I am having a lot of fun at camp this summer. All the counselors and campers have Native American names. My counselor, Sitting Bull, suggested three names that he thought I might like to be called. His **proposal** for *White Cloud* intrigued me, so I chose that one. There is so much to do here that I am never bored. My favorite activity is archery. The campers were divided into **classifications**, depending on their experience. I am in the novice group, called Papoose. At first, I just shot arrows toward the target. Sitting Bull helped me realize that there is actual skill involved. I learned how to place the **V-shaped cut** at the end of the arrow into the bowstring, pull back until the bowstring is **stretched tightly**, let my fingers roll off the string, and remain still until the arrow reaches the target. I am amazed at how the **act of being stretched to stiffness** of the bow is what propels the arrow forward. It is amazing how much strength it actually takes to do archery! When everyone's **long, narrow case for carrying or holding arrows** is empty, then we are allowed to take a closer look at our targets and collect our arrows. I hope I can get a bull's-eye before camp is over on Saturday!

  The food has been really good here at camp. For dinner, I ate a **sandwich consisting of a ground beef patty on a round bun**, and enjoyed a **rolled pastry made from thin dough that contains a filling** for dessert. Tonight we are going to roast marshmallows around a campfire and make s'mores. I really enjoy the campfire each night because we share about how God is working in each of our lives. There have been three campers who gave their lives to Christ. It is so awesome to see the next **group of people born at approximately the same time** become believers. I will see you on Saturday.

  Love,
  Phillip

Pattern Words
diesel
seltzer
strudel
pretzel
edelweiss
liverwurst
gesundheit
sauerkraut
hamburger
frankfurter
delicatessen
pumpernickel

Content Words
taut
notch
quiver
tension
graphite
concentric
categories

Vocabulary Words
generation
regenerate
exposition
proposition

1. _____ 2. _____ 3. _____
4. _____ 5. _____ 6. _____
7. _____ 8. _____ 9. _____

10. On a separate piece of paper, write a letter home describing your imaginative adventures at an archery camp.

Name _____

35.2
Word Analysis
Words from Asian Languages

Pattern Words
futon
aikido
bonsai
karate
teriyaki
kung fu
gung ho
chopsticks
chow mein
veranda
pajamas
bungalow

Many words in the English language originally came from Asian languages. Knowledge of word origins helps in building spelling and vocabulary skills.

The first five Pattern Words are derived from Japanese. The next four words are derived from Chinese. The last three words are derived from Hindi, which is spoken in India.

Write Pattern Words to complete the exercises. Sort the words by derivation.

1.–3. Words from Hindi   4.–7. Words from Chinese
8.–12. Words from Japanese

1. _____   2. _____
3. _____   4. _____
5. _____   6. _____
7. _____   8. _____
9. _____   10. _____
11. _____   12. _____

Write Content Words to complete the exercises.

13. Each martial art is a m_____, individual sport.
14. To solve the d_____ of categorizing a martial art, it is either in a striking or grappling category.
15. P_____ of martial arts learn self-defense skills.
16. Discipline and exercise are benefits of p_____ in martial arts training.
17. Each sport has its own d_____ features. Kung fu features a series of r_____ movements.
18. Aikido students take tests of c_____ to advance in rank.

Content Words
dilemma
rhythmic
distinctive
methodical
competency
participation
practitioners

Vocabulary Words
disgrace
gracious
specialize
specialty

Challenge Words
_____
_____

martial arts

35.2 Vocabulary: Words from Asian Languages

Prefix		Root		Suffix	
dis-	not	grac	pleasing, thankful	-ious	quality of
		spec	kind	-ial	related to
				-ize	to make
				-ty	state of

Pattern Words
futon
aikido
bonsai
karate
teriyaki
kung fu
gung ho
chopsticks
chow mein
veranda
pajamas
bungalow

Write the Vocabulary Words.

1. _____ 2. _____
3. _____ 4. _____

Refer to the table to complete the exercises. Write the word that is being defined.

5. marked by pleasantness and courtesy _____
6. not pleasing others; to bring shame _____
7. a state of expertise in one kind of activity _____
8. making a concentrated study in one kind of activity _____

Write Vocabulary Words to complete the sentences.

9. Sensei /'sen sā/ Mariko Yasumura's _____ is karate.

10. At the beginning of each class, Sensei Mariko makes a _____ and respectful bow to her students.

11. Sensei Mariko is a traditional karate teacher. She teaches her students to _____ in the sequence of movements of the *kata* /'kä tä/, which are training exercises.

12. Sensei Mariko will not allow any student to _____ any other student by making demeaning remarks.

Content Words
dilemma
rhythmic
distinctive
methodical
competency
participation
practitioners

Vocabulary Words
disgrace
gracious
specialize
specialty

Choose the best meaning for each underlined word.

13. Mr. Fujiwara trimmed his <u>bonsai</u> and bound the branches with wire.
    ○ bushes   ○ flowers   ○ decorative dwarf plant or tree

14. He keeps his bonsai on the <u>veranda</u>.
    ○ covered patio   ○ low building   ○ window sill

15. Mr. Fujiwara's miniature trees are no taller than <u>chopsticks</u>.
    ○ a house   ○ a ruler   ○ two sticks used to pick up food

Name _____

35.3

Word Study Strategies
Words from Asian Languages

Look up **aikido**, **karate**, and **kung fu** in the Spelling Dictionary. Choose the best word for each line. Write the words.

1. _____ uses kicks or blocks for self-defense, _____ employs locks and holds to overpower an opponent, and _____ features weapons.

Look up **teriyaki** and **chow mein** in the Spelling Dictionary. Choose the best word for each line. Write the words.

2. Dae enjoyed _____ chicken marinated in soy sauce with a side dish of _____.

A complex sentence is a combination of an independent and a dependent clause. A dependent clause may begin with a subordinating conjunction, such as *after*, *although*, *as*, *because*, *since*, *when*, *where*, and *while*.

Read each set of two clauses. Combine the clauses into a complex sentence that makes sense, beginning with either the independent or dependent clause. Use a comma after a dependent clause that begins a sentence.

3. Jin Ho pulled his futon onto the veranda

   the rain had stopped

   _____

   _____

4. Lana proved her competency in kung fu

   she received her black belt

   _____

   _____

5. they have studied it for years

   karate masters specialize in karate

   _____

   _____

6. they practice the rhythmic movements

   participants learn the *kata*

   _____

   _____

Pattern Words
futon
aikido
bonsai
karate
teriyaki
kung fu
gung ho
chopsticks
chow mein
veranda
pajamas
bungalow

Content Words
dilemma
rhythmic
distinctive
methodical
competency
participation
practitioners

Vocabulary Words
disgrace
gracious
specialize
specialty

© Spelling Plus Grade 6

Refer to the Spelling Dictionary.

35.4
Writing Words from Asian Languages

Pattern Words
futon
aikido
bonsai
karate
teriyaki
kung fu
gung ho
chopsticks
chow mein
veranda
pajamas
bungalow

Content Words
dilemma
rhythmic
distinctive
methodical
competency
participation
practitioners

Vocabulary Words
disgrace
gracious
specialize
specialty

Use words derived from Japanese to complete the sentences.

Genji and the Kite

Little Genji rubbed his sleepy eyes as he sat up on his _____. Today was the annual Festival of Cranes. Contests in martial arts, displays of ornate _____, and vendors selling delicious _____ meats would be a part of the festival. Genji longed to see a match of _____ and watch wrestlers practice _____, but his mother said that he was too little to go. Genji sadly slipped outside to fly his kite. Soon there was no string left; still the kite rose into the sky. Genji could not bear to lose his kite, so he let the wind lift him from the ground. He flew high enough to see the sights of the festival below. Soon the wind set Genji down, whereupon he ran to tell his mother all about the festival.

Use words derived from Chinese to complete the sentences.

Jun

Jun was a servant of Master Ju Long, an expert in the art of _____. Jun longed to study kung fu, but because he was only a servant, he was forbidden to learn the art. As he sat eating a bowl of _____, he pretended that one of his _____ was a tiny staff and mimicked the rhythmic *tai chi* that he had seen the master practice many times before. He was unaware that Master Ju Long was watching, amazed by Jun's mastery of the movements. Master Ju Long consented to teach Jun, and Jun eventually became a great kung-fu master. He was always teaching those less fortunate, but willing to learn.

Use words derived from Hindi to complete the sentences.

A Cricket's Tale

Princess Anju could not sleep because the night was too hot. Her silk _____ were damp with perspiration. So, she went out of her _____ to cool herself. There, on the _____, Princess Anju met a cricket. She commanded the cricket to use his wings as fans to cool her. Although he did his best, the cricket could not manage a breeze, only a chirp. You may still hear him on summer nights, trying to please the princess.

Name _____

36.1

Review Chapters 31–35
Chapter 31

Pattern Words

Chapter 31 Frequently Misspelled Words	Chapter 32 Words from French and Italian	Chapter 33 Words from Spanish	Chapter 34 Words from German	Chapter 35 Words from Asian Languages
privilege	ballet	fiesta	diesel	futon
definitely	bouquet	guitar	seltzer	aikido
sincerely	gourmet	maize	strudel	bonsai
miniature	etiquette	tortilla	pretzel	karate
necessary	chauffeur	alfalfa	edelweiss	teriyaki
separately	chandelier	pronto	liverwurst	kung fu
meticulous	finale	burrito	gesundheit	gung ho
restaurant	adagio	anchovy	sauerkraut	chopsticks
conscientious	rotunda	mariachi	hamburger	chow mein
embarrassed	parapet	enchilada	frankfurter	veranda
perseverance	spaghetti	quesadilla	delicatessen	pajamas
congratulations	macaroni	sombrero	pumpernickel	bungalow

Content Words

divot	poised	feint	taut	dilemma
torque	exhibition	bout	notch	rhythmic
titanium	dressage	torso	quiver	distinctive
hazards	obstacles	tactics	tension	methodical
accuracy	equestrian	initiated	graphite	competency
trajectory	prestigious	posture	concentric	participation
maintenance	domesticated	dexterity	categories	practitioners

Vocabulary Words

dignify	auction	clarity	generation	disgrace
dignity	auctioneer	declaration	regenerate	gracious
sociable	circumspectly	detection	exposition	specialize
society	circumvent	protected	proposition	specialty

Read Chapter 31 Pattern Words. Follow the directions given.

1. Circle the four words that contain three syllables.
2. Underline the seven words that contain four syllables.
3. Box in the word that contains five syllables.
4. Write the words that contain double s.

   _____   _____

5. Write the words that end in -ly.

   _____   _____   _____

Write the missing letters to complete the words from French.

1. ch __ __ f __ __ __ r
2. b __ __ q __ __ __
3. __ o __ __ m __ __
4. __ a __ l __ __
5. c __ a n __ e l __ __ r
6. e t __ q __ __ t __ e

Write the missing letters to complete the words from Italian.

7. s p __ g __ __ t __ i
8. __ a c __ r __ __ __
9. a __ a __ __ __
10. f __ n __ __ __
11. __ a __ a __ e __
12. __ o t __ n __ __

ballet
bouquet
gourmet
etiquette
chauffeur
chandelier
finale
adagio
rotunda
parapet
spaghetti
macaroni

Review Chapters 31–35
Chapters 32–33

36.2

Find the words from Spanish in the word search. Circle the words and write them on the lines. The words go across, down, diagonally, and backwards. Some of the words share letters.

fiesta
guitar
maize
tortilla
alfalfa
pronto
burrito
anchovy
mariachi
enchilada
quesadilla
sombrero

```
p b y d u p b t y d o u p b y e
d s o m b r e r o t n o r p n u
p b a y i h c a i r a m d c u p
u y t b d r l r p b t y h d u y
m p s b a f r y d u y i p b d u
y a e t a u p b y d l u l p p d
p y i l b q u e s a d i l l a u
d u f z z p y d d u b y d u a p
g a f z e b u a n c h o v y v y
```

_____   _____   _____

_____   _____   _____

_____   _____   _____

_____   _____   _____

142

Name _____

36.3

Review Chapters 31–35
Chapters 34–35

Read each word. Decide if it is spelled correctly or incorrectly. Fill in the circle. Write each word correctly.

		Correct	Incorrect	
1.	pretzel	○	○	_____
2.	sourkraut	○	○	_____
3.	edelweis	○	○	_____
4.	pumpernickel	○	○	_____
5.	deisel	○	○	_____
6.	delicatesen	○	○	_____
7.	hamberger	○	○	_____
8.	liverwerst	○	○	_____
9.	seltser	○	○	_____
10.	frankfurter	○	○	_____
11.	gesundheit	○	○	_____
12.	struedel	○	○	_____

diesel
seltzer
strudel
pretzel
edelweiss
liverwurst
gesundheit
sauerkraut
hamburger
frankfurter
delicatessen
pumpernickel

Write a word from an Asian language in each shape box. The blue shape boxes indicate Japanese words. The orange shape boxes indicate Chinese words. The purple boxes indicate Hindi words.

futon
aikido
bonsai
karate
teriyaki
kung fu
gung ho
chopsticks
chow mein
veranda
pajamas
bungalow

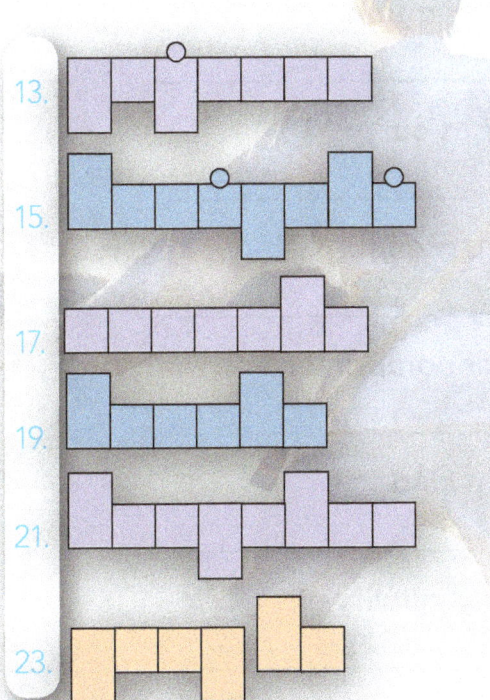

143

Unscramble each Content Word and write it correctly.

1. ttccasi _____
2. crncocneti _____
3. partnioiiatpc _____
4. xyditreet _____
5. dmsiaedtcteo _____
6. neaqieruts _____
7. nitscarorepit _____
8. shraadz _____
9. lihmeoatdc _____
10. siigtrupsoe _____
11. jyrorcetta _____
12. enntimcaena _____
13. iaieitdtn _____
14. gaistrcoee _____

Review Chapters 31–35
Content and Vocabulary Words

hazards
trajectory
maintenance
equestrian
prestigious
domesticated
tactics
initiated
dexterity
tension
concentric
categories
methodical
participation
practitioners

Write the missing affix or root to complete each Vocabulary Word.
Write each word. Complete each definition with the missing affix or root.

dignify
sociable
society
auction
circumspectly
circumvent
declaration
detection
protected
generation
regenerate
exposition
gracious
specialize
specialty

15. _____ generate _____
The prefix _____ means **again**.

16. _____ position _____
The prefix _____ means **out of**.

17. _____ spectly _____
The root _____ means **around**.

18. _____ ety _____
The root _____ means **companion**.

19. _____ ialize _____
The root _____ means **kind**.

20. grac _____ _____
The suffix _____ means **quality of**.

21. declar _____ _____
The suffix _____ means **state of**.

144

Word Bank

Name _____

A *a* _____

B *B* _____

basketball

C *C*

canoeing

D *D*

E *E*

F *F*

G *G*

H *H*

horseback riding

I *I*

J *J*

K *K*

karate

L *L*

M *m*

motocross

N *n*

O o

P p

pole vault

Q q

R *R*

S *S*

surfing

T *T*

U *u*

V *v*

W *w*

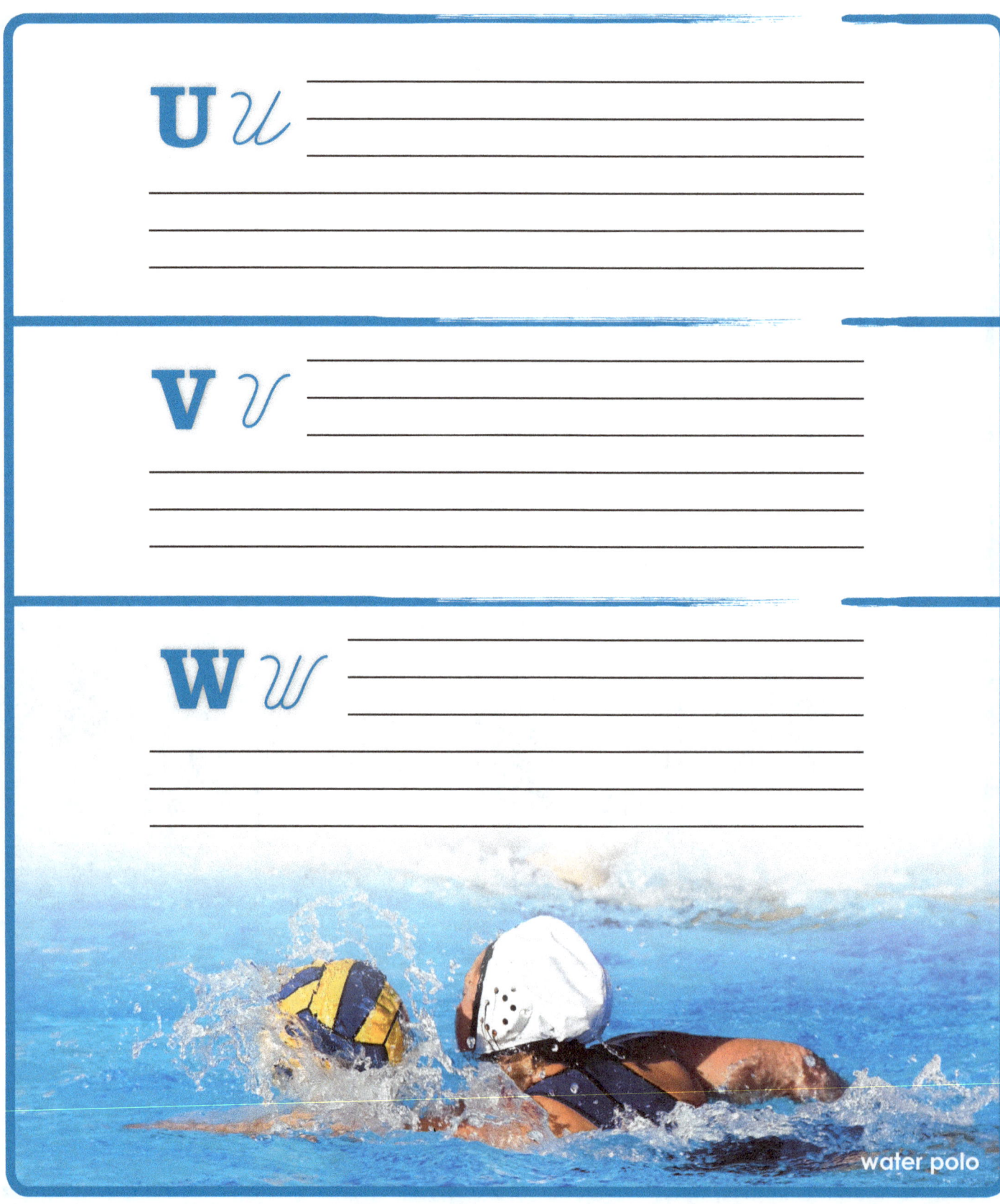

water polo

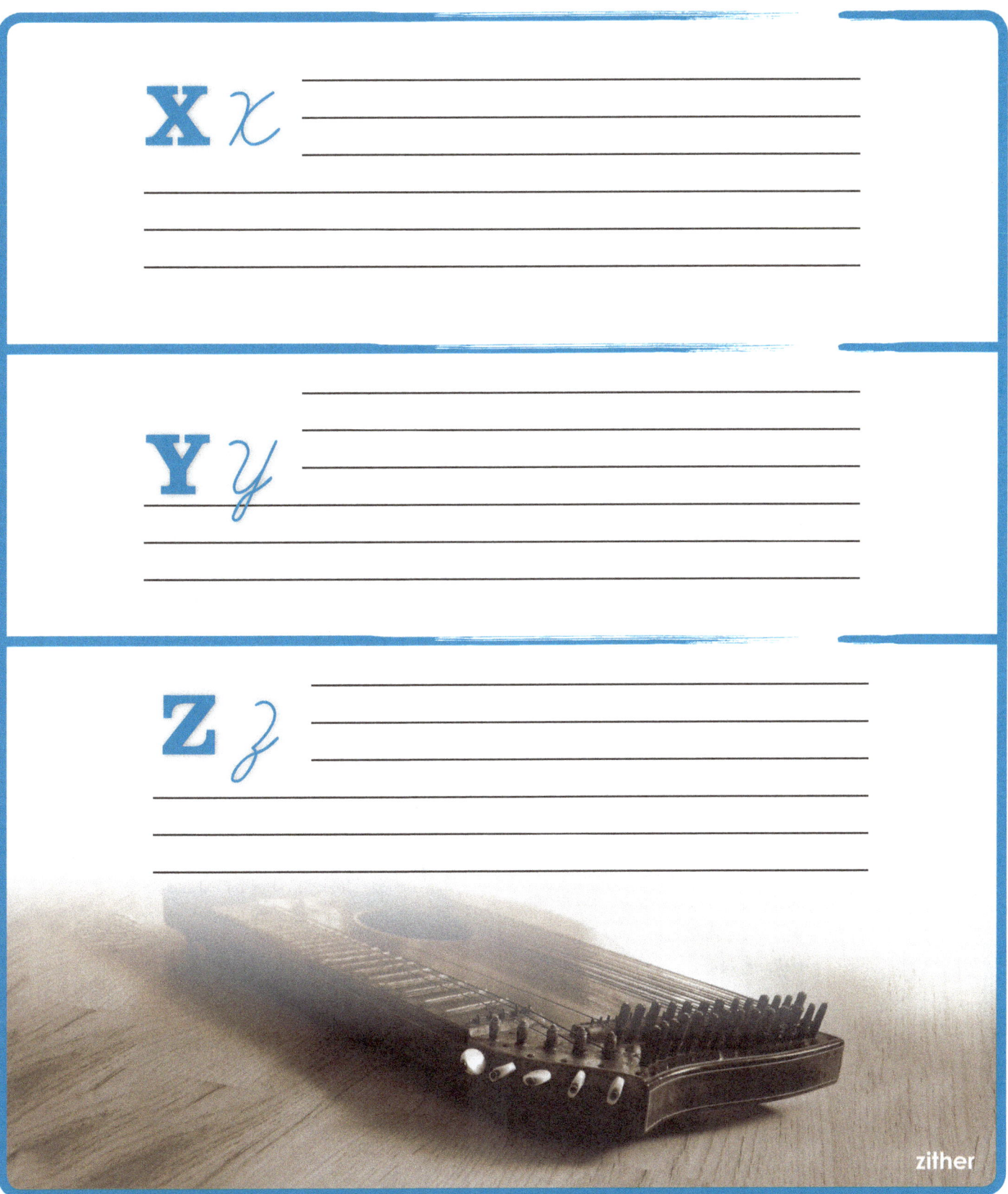

zither

Pronunciation Key

Letters written within slashes on this key represent common phonemes, the smallest units of distinct sound in English. Listed to the right are variant spellings for these sounds.

Consonants

/b/	**b**i**b**, **b**a**b**y, **bu**bb**le
/ch/	**ch**ild, mu**ch**, pa**tch**, na**t**ure, ques**t**ion
/d/	**d**ay, sa**d**, la**dd**er
/f/	**f**ish, o**f**ten, o**ff**, **ph**one, cou**gh**
/g/	**g**o, bi**g**, wi**gg**le, **gh**ost, lea**gue**
/h/	**h**ot, **h**urry, **wh**o
/j/	**j**ump, **j**u**dg**e, **g**ym, ran**ge**
/k/	**k**eep, **c**up, si**ck**, ti**ck**le, pi**c**nic, anti**que**, **sch**ool
/l/	**l**ook, ta**ll**, **l**i**l**y, a**ll**ey, penci**l**
/m/	**m**y, co**me**, **m**o**mm**y
/n/	**n**o, **n**i**ne**, wi**nn**er, **kn**ow
/ng/	ri**ng**, si**ng**ing
/p/	**p**ie, ho**pe**, a**pp**le
/kw/	**qu**een, **qu**iet, **ch**oir
/r/	**r**ed, **r**ose, nea**r**, a**rr**ow
/s/	**s**ee, le**ss**on, mi**ss**, **c**ity, dan**ce**
/sh/	**sh**e, wi**sh**, **s**ugar, ma**ch**ine, na**t**ion, spe**c**ial
/t/	**t**ie, ea**t**, **t**a**tt**le, walk**ed**
/th/	**th**ink, bo**th** (breath)
/<u>th</u>/	**th**is, ei**th**er (voice)
/v/	**v**ase, sa**ve**
/w/	**w**e, **w**ell
/hw/ or /w/	**wh**at, **wh**y, **wh**ether
/y/	**y**es, **y**ellow, on**i**on, mill**i**on
/z/	**z**oo, fu**zz**y, ma**ze**, ha**s**
/zh/	mea**s**ure, vi**s**ion

Vowels

/ā/	**a**ble, d**a**te, **ai**d, p**ay**, **eigh**t, gr**ea**t
/a/	p**a**t, **a**pple
/ä/	f**a**ther (same sound as /o/)
/är/	f**ar**m, **ar**m, sp**ar**kle, h**ear**t
/ē/	m**e**, b**ee**, m**ea**t, ch**ie**f, c**ei**ling, lad**y**, vall**ey**
/e/	b**e**t, **e**dge, m**e**ss, r**ea**dy, fr**ie**nd
/ī/	**I**, f**i**ne, n**igh**t, p**ie**, b**y**
/i/	h**i**s, **i**t, g**y**m
/ō/	b**o**ne, **o**pen, c**oa**t, sh**ow**, s**ou**l
/o/	t**o**p, **o**tter, b**o**ther (same sound as /ä/)
/ȯ/	s**o**ft, **o**ften, **a**lso, h**au**l, c**augh**t, dr**aw**, b**ough**t
/oi/	j**oy**, f**oi**l, r**oy**al
/oo/	b**oo**k, p**u**ll, sh**ou**ld
/o͞o/	p**oo**l, t**u**be, t**o**, st**ew**, fr**ui**t, gr**ou**p
/yo͞o/	**u**se, f**ue**l, p**ew**, **you**, b**eau**ty
/ou/	**ou**t, n**ow**, t**ow**el
/u/	h**u**t, l**o**ve, c**ou**ple, an**o**ther (used in stressed syllables)
/âr/	**air**, c**are**, b**ear**, Janu**ary**
/ôr/	f**or**, t**or**n, c**or**n, ch**ore**, w**ar**m
/îr/	**ear**, p**ier**ce, w**eir**d
/ûr/	t**ur**n, w**or**d, th**ir**d, t**ur**tle, f**er**tile, h**ear**d (used in stressed syllables)
	f**ur**ther, col**or** (used in unstressed syllables)
/ə/	schwa—the /u/ sound in unstressed syllables:
	alike
	sudd**e**n
	penc**i**l
	cott**o**n
	circ**u**s

Spelling Dictionary

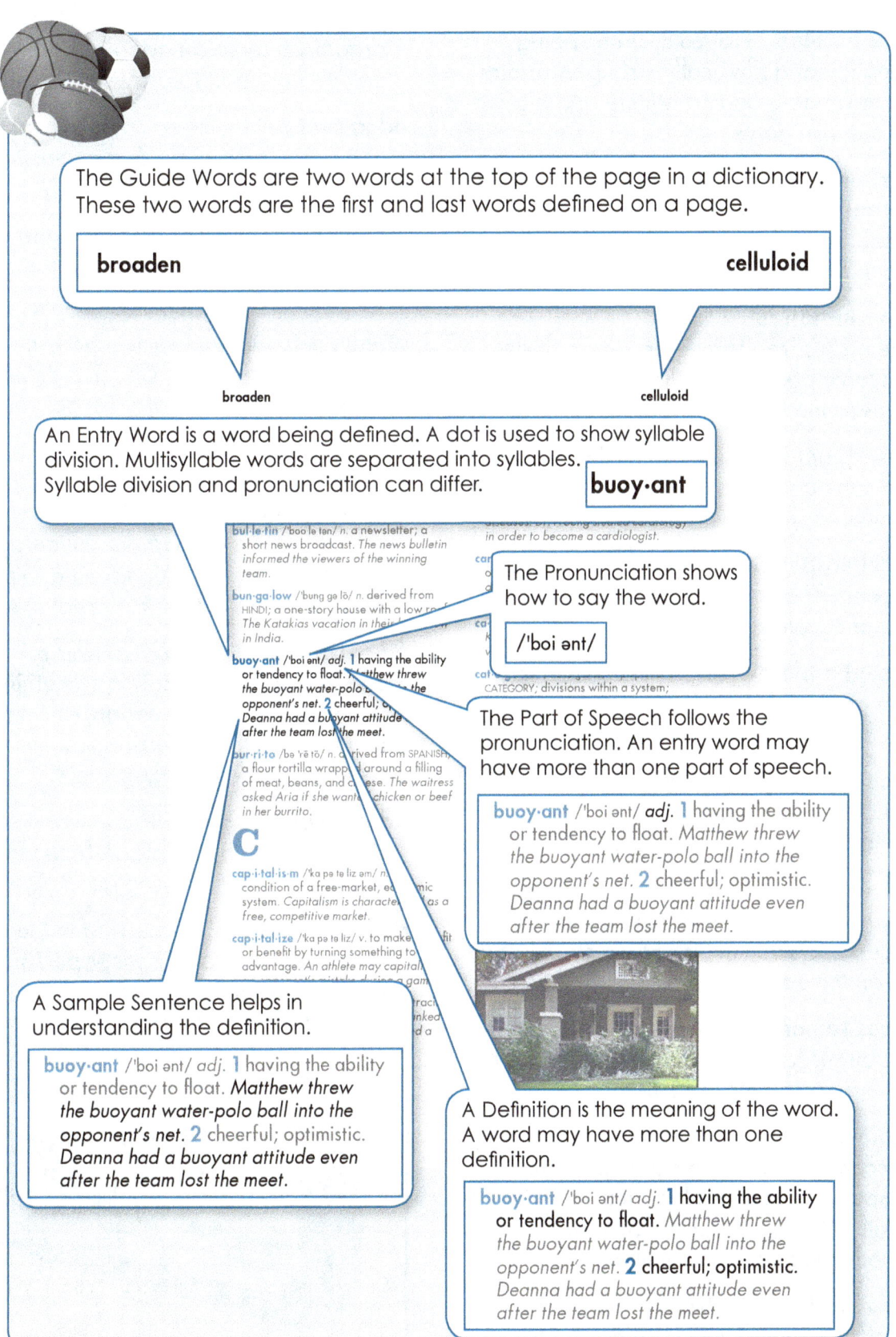

The Guide Words are two words at the top of the page in a dictionary. These two words are the first and last words defined on a page.

broaden   celluloid

An Entry Word is a word being defined. A dot is used to show syllable division. Multisyllable words are separated into syllables. Syllable division and pronunciation can differ.

buoy·ant

The Pronunciation shows how to say the word.

/ˈbɔɪ ənt/

The Part of Speech follows the pronunciation. An entry word may have more than one part of speech.

buoy·ant /ˈbɔɪ ənt/ *adj.* **1** having the ability or tendency to float. *Matthew threw the buoyant water-polo ball into the opponent's net.* **2** cheerful; optimistic. *Deanna had a buoyant attitude even after the team lost the meet.*

A Sample Sentence helps in understanding the definition.

buoy·ant /ˈbɔɪ ənt/ *adj.* **1** having the ability or tendency to float. *Matthew threw the buoyant water-polo ball into the opponent's net.* **2** cheerful; optimistic. *Deanna had a buoyant attitude even after the team lost the meet.*

A Definition is the meaning of the word. A word may have more than one definition.

buoy·ant /ˈbɔɪ ənt/ *adj.* **1** having the ability or tendency to float. *Matthew threw the buoyant water-polo ball into the opponent's net.* **2** cheerful; optimistic. *Deanna had a buoyant attitude even after the team lost the meet.*

A

a·ble-bod·ied /ā bəl 'bo dēd/ *adj.* being healthy and physically strong. *Marlene was an able-bodied athlete and played in the entire game.*

a·brupt·ly /ə 'brupt lē/ *adv.* in a sudden breaking away; suddenly. *The track meet was ended abruptly by a sudden thunderstorm.*

ab·so·lu·tion /ab sə 'loo shən/ *n.* state of being set free from blame or guilt. *We receive absolution when we confess our sins to the Lord.*

ab·sorb·ent /əb 'sôr bənt/ *adj.* the tendency to soak up. *Myra used an absorbent towel to soak up the water on the seats.*

ac·cel·er·ates /ik 'se lə rāts/ *v.* increases in speed. *The skier rises on her skis as the boat accelerates.*

ac·cept·a·ble /ik 'sep tə bəl/ *adj.* able to be accepted. *The bronze medal was acceptable to the track coach.*

ac·co·lades /'a kə lādz/ *n. pl.* plural of ACCOLADE; praises. *Could you hear the announcer over the accolades of the fans?*

ac·cu·ra·cy /'a kyə rə sē/ *n.* precision. *Vern used accuracy in his putting stroke and won the golf tournament.*

ac·cus·tomed /ə 'kus təmd/ *adj.* being in the habit; usual. *The team is accustomed to playing on their home field.*

a·chieve·ment /ə 'chēv mənt/ *n.* a state of accomplishment; an accomplishment, especially as a result of unusual effort or skill. *Wendy's technical achievement in the high jump was admirable.*

ac·ro·ba·tics /a krə 'ba tiks/ *n.* a spectacular performance demonstrating agility or complexity. *A diver implements acrobatics into his or her routine.*

a·da·gio /ə 'dä zhē ō/ *n.* derived from ITALIAN; a musical composition usually performed at a slow tempo. *As the organist played an adagio, Carmen bowed her head to pray.*

ad·ja·cent /ə 'jā sənt/ *adj.* nearby; connected at a point; adjoining. *Our campsite was adjacent to the dock.*

ad·join·ing /ə 'joi ning/ *adj.* joining at a point or a line. *The soccer field and the skate park are adjoining.*

ad·min·is·tra·tor /əd 'mi nə strā tûr/ *n.* director; supervisor. *Coach Preston was the school administrator for sporting events.*

ad·van·tage /əd 'van tij/ *n.* **1** the first point in tennis after a deuce. *Lena's confidence rose when she earned the advantage in tennis.* **2** a benefit. *An advantage to playing tennis is that it is great exercise.*

ad·ver·tise·ment /ad vûr 'tiz mənt/ *n.* a public notice promoting something in a newspaper, on television, or on radio. *Did you see the advertisement for field hockey in today's newspaper?*

ad·vis·a·ble /əd 'vi zə bəl/ *adj.* worth doing; recommendable. *A face mask is advisable when playing goalkeeper.*

ae·ri·al /'âr ē əl/ *adj.* occurring in the air above the surface. *Spencer performed an aerial trick on his wakeboard.*

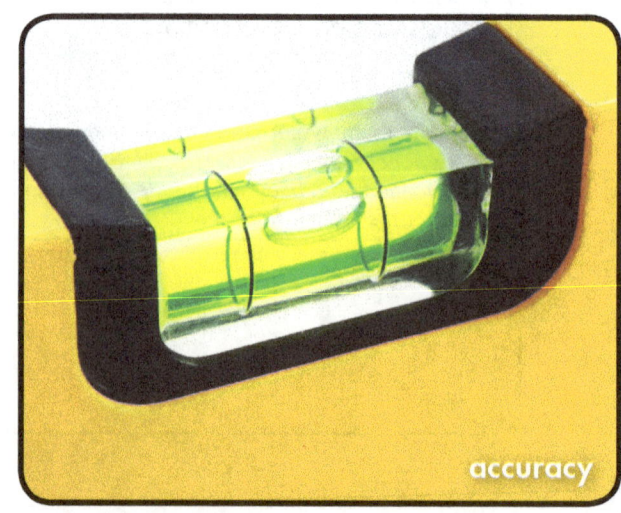
accuracy

aer·o·bic /er ˈō bik/ *adj.* increasing oxygen consumption in the body. *The doctor suggested that Kaylin begin an aerobic sport such as tennis.*

ag·gres·sive /ə ˈgre siv/ *adj.* hostile. *The Hawks played a very aggressive team last week.*

a·ghast /ə ˈgast/ *adj.* horrified; astonished. *The crowd was aghast when the soccer player broke her ankle.*

a·gile /ˈa jəl/ *adj.* having the ability to move quickly; able to move quickly. *The agile rider could maneuver her bike around sharp corners.*

a·gil·i·ty /ə ˈji lə tē/ *n.* the ability to move quickly. *Surfing requires agility.*

ai·ki·do /ī ki ˈdō/ *n.* derived from JAPANESE; a martial art using locks and holds. *Aikido is a martial art that originated in Japan.*

al·fal·fa /al ˈfal fə/ *n.* derived from SPANISH; a plant from the pea family that is grown for hay and forage; a legume. *Papá Valdez feeds alfalfa to the livestock on his farm.*

al·ge·bra /ˈal jə brə/ *adj.* the branch of mathematics where symbols are used to represent unknown numbers. *Tavonia did her algebra homework before soccer practice.*

al·ter·a·tion /ȯl tə ˈrā shən/ *n.* the state of changing partly, but not into some other form; modification. *Candice made an alteration to the length of her sleeves.*

al·tered /ˈȯl tûrd/ *v.* past tense of ALTER; changed partly, but not into some other form. *The girls' team altered their uniforms by hemming their shorts.*

al·ter·nates /ˈȯl tûr nāts/ *v.* follows in succession; fluctuates. *In table tennis, each player alternates hitting the ball.*

a·lu·mi·num /ə ˈlo͞o mə nəm/ *adj.* a soft, silver-white metal. *Many players use aluminum badminton rackets.*

am·a·teur /ˈa mə chûr/ *adj.* lacking in experience. *Ivan is an amateur player who is dreaming of becoming a professional.*

am·bi·tion /am ˈbi shən/ *n.* the desire to achieve. *Zeke's ambition is to become a champion surfer.*

an·chored /ˈang kûrd/ *v.* past tense of ANCHOR; to have secured firmly. *A portaledge is a tent that is anchored to the side of a rock.*

an·cho·vy /ˈan chō vē/ *n.* derived from SPANISH; a small fish. *Have you ever eaten an anchovy?*

an·gu·lar /ˈang gyə lûr/ *adj.* sharply defined; thin. *Many track-and-field athletes are lean and have angular features.*

an·nounce·ments /ə ˈnount smənts/ *n. pl.* plural of ANNOUNCEMENT; public statements; written notices. *Al heard the announcements about the Nordic skiing event.*

an·ti·bi·ot·ics /an ti bī ˈo tiks/ *n. pl.* plural of ANTIBIOTIC; medication against harmful biological organisms. *Antibiotics are sometimes prescribed for infections.*

an·tic·i·pate /an ˈti sə pāt/ *v.* to expect or look forward to; to deal with something beforehand. *A motocross racer should anticipate racing in all types of weather.*

an·ti·quat·ed /ˈan tə kwā təd/ *v.* past tense of ANTIQUATE; to cause to be old or outdated. *The new soccer stadium's layout antiquated the older stadium's design.*

an·ti·stress /an tī ˈstres/ *adj.* that which works against stress. *Proper rest and nutrition are antistress strategies for health.*

anx·ious /ˈangk shəs/ *adj.* worried. *The teammates were anxious when one of the players was injured.*

a·pol·o·gy /ə ˈpo lə jē/ *n.* a statement expressing remorse and regret. *An apology was due after unsportsmanlike conduct was exhibited.*

ap·par·ent /ə ˈpâr ənt/ *adj.* inclined to appear; visible; obvious. *It is apparent that Marcus has a God-given talent for swimming.*

ap·pli·cant /ˈa pli kənt/ *n.* a person who applies for a job; candidate. *The applicant turned in his application for the new position.*

a·qua·tics /ə ˈkwä tiks/ *n. pl.* plural of AQUATIC; water sports. *Aquatics include swimming and diving.*

ar·bi·trar·y /ˈär bə trâr ē/ *adj.* related to a personal decision or judgment; random. *In recreational tennis, players make arbitrary decisions.*

ar·bi·trate /ˈär bə trāt/ *v.* to act as a judge to make a decision. *Line judges arbitrate disputes over where the ball landed.*

ar·chi·tec·tur·al /är kə ˈtek chə rəl/ *adj.* relating to a single design, form, or structure. *Building an ice rink can be an architectural challenge.*

a·re·nas /ə ˈrē nəz/ *n. pl.* plural of ARENA; enclosed stadiums. *Basketball is played in arenas throughout the world.*

ar·range·ment /ə ˈrānj mənt/ *n.* a state of placement or order. *Rita noticed the arrangement of the landing mats in the pole-vault pit.*

as·cend·ing /ə ˈsen ding/ *v.* rising to a higher level. *The climbers will be ascending the mountain for two days.*

as·pi·ra·tion /as pə ˈrā shən/ *n.* a state of desiring to achieve a goal; a hope. *My aspiration is to become like Jesus.*

as·sis·tance /ə ˈsis tənts/ *n.* help. *We required assistance to restart the stalled boat.*

as·so·ci·a·tion /ə sō sē ˈā shən/ *n.* organization; group. *The amateur soccer association voted on the yearly budget.*

ath·lete /ˈath lēt/ *n.* a person skilled in playing sports. *An athlete trains hard to improve his or her skills.*

at·ti·tude /ˈa tə tōōd/ *n.* one's thoughts or feelings about something. *Ryan's attitude improved when he took time to pray.*

auc·tion /ˈȯk shən/ *n.* a sale using bids to increase the price of each item. *The thoroughbred was sold at auction to the highest bidder.*

auc·tion·eer /ȯk shə ˈnîr/ *n.* one who asks for an increase in bidding. *The auctioneer sold a palomino to Mrs. Chavez.*

au·to·graphed /ˈȯ tə grafd/ *v.* past tense of AUTOGRAPH; to have written a signature with one's own hand. *Micah autographed the fan's racquetball program after the match.*

au·to·mo·bile /ˈȯ tə mō bēl/ *n.* a vehicle designed to transport passengers. *Lorell rode in an antique automobile to the game banquet.*

au·to·mo·tive /ȯ tə ˈmō tiv/ *adj.* relating to automobiles. *The attendees of the automotive convention played racquetball daily.*

a·vail·a·bil·i·ty /ə vā lə ˈbi lə tē/ *n.* accessibility; the condition of being accessible or available. *What is your availability for track-and-field practice this week?*

awe·some /ˈȯ səm/ *adj.* terrific. *Our God is absolutely awesome!*

awk·ward /ˈȯ kwûrd/ *adj.* clumsy, not graceful; embarrassing. *Sometimes rock climbers have awkward maneuvers.*

axles

ax·les /ˈak səlz/ *n. pl.* plural of AXLE; bars with bearings at their ends on which wheels revolve. *The axles help hold the wheels on skateboards and in-line skates.*

B

back·ache /ˈbak āk/ *n.* a pain affecting the back. *Becka had a backache after being kicked by another player.*

bal·anc·ing /ˈba lənt sing/ *v.* maintaining physical equilibrium. *Nate is balancing on only one ski.*

bal·let /ba ˈlā/ *n.* derived from FRENCH; a form of dance originating in France. *The gait of the Tennessee walking horse resembles ballet.*

ba·sis /ˈbā səs/ *n.* the foundation. *Motorcycle cross-country riding became the basis for BMX.*

beach·comb·ing /ˈbēch kō ming/ *v.* looking for or collecting useful items from the beach. *Reno and Austin are beachcombing in Laguna Niguel.*

beau·ti·ful·ly /ˈbyo͞o ti fə lē/ *adv.* attractively. *Our wonderful world was beautifully designed by our loving God.*

be·hav·ior /bi ˈhā vyər/ *n.* the manner or way of conducting oneself; conduct. *The volleyball player's behavior was exemplary.*

be·liev·ers /bə ˈlē vûrz/ *n. pl.* plural of BELIEVER; people who have strong firm opinions as in religious beliefs. *Believers in Christ have the promise of eternal salvation.*

ben·e·fi·cial /be nə ˈfi shəl/ *adj.* that which improves one's well-being. *Basketball and other aerobic sports are beneficial to one's health.*

brilliant

ben·e·fit·ted /ˈbe nə fi təd/ *v.* past tense of BENEFIT; to have given someone help or an advantage. *Tarah benefitted from hours of practice on the racecourse.*

bi·lin·gual /bī ˈling gwəl/ *adj.* related to speaking two languages. *The new coach was bilingual and was able to communicate effectively.*

bon·sai /ˈbon sī/ *n.* **1** derived from JAPANESE; a decorative dwarf plant or tree. *Jia trains her bonsai to look like a windblown cypress tree.* *n. pl.* **2** plural of BONSAI; decorative dwarf plants or trees. *Mr. Yamamoto has a display of ten bonsai in the window of his flower shop.*

boul·der·ing /ˈbōl də ring/ *n.* rock climbing. *Lani and her family enjoy bouldering on weekends.*

bound·a·ries /ˈboun də rēz/ *n. pl.* plural of BOUNDARY; limits. *Line judges determine if the ball lands outside the boundaries.*

bou·quet /bō ˈkā/ *n.* derived from FRENCH; a grouping of flowers often held in one's hand. *Nina presented a bouquet to the winner of the steeplechase.*

bout /ˈbout/ *n.* an athletic match. *Mahera played a three-minute bout with Tamar.*

bril·liant /ˈbril yənt/ *adj.* having great ability; very smart; talented. *Misty exhibited brilliant technique on the court.*

bouldering

broad·en /ˈbrȯ dən/ v. to widen. *The game was so close that the coach wanted to broaden the score.*

bro·chure /brō ˈshoor/ n. pamphlet. *Our coach gave my teammates and me a brochure for hockey camp.*

bul·le·tin /ˈboo lə tən/ n. a newsletter; a short news broadcast. *The news bulletin informed the viewers of the winning team.*

bun·ga·low /ˈbung gə lō/ n. derived from HINDI; a one-story house with a low roof. *The Katakias vacation in their bungalow in India.*

buoy·ant /ˈboi ənt/ adj. **1** having the ability or tendency to float. *Matthew threw the buoyant water-polo ball into the opponent's net.* **2** cheerful; optimistic. *Deanna had a buoyant attitude even after the team lost the meet.*

bur·ri·to /bə ˈrē tō/ n. derived from SPANISH; a flour tortilla wrapped around a filling of meat, beans, and cheese. *The waitress asked Aria if she wanted chicken or beef in her burrito.*

C

cap·i·tal·is·m /ˈka pə tə liz əm/ n. the condition of a free-market, economic system. *Capitalism is characterized as a free, competitive market.*

cap·i·tal·ize /ˈka pə tə liz/ v. to make a profit or benefit by turning something to an advantage. *An athlete may capitalize on an opponent's mistake during a game.*

car·di·o·gram /ˈkär dē ə gram/ n. the tracing made by a cardiograph. *Zane thanked the Lord that a cardiogram showed a normal heartbeat.*

car·di·o·graph /ˈkär dē ə graf/ n. an instrument that measures the movements of the heart. *The patient was connected to the cardiograph by wires.*

car·di·ol·o·gy /kär dē ˈo lə jē/ n. the study of the heart and treatment of disorders and diseases. *Dr. Froelig studied cardiology in order to become a cardiologist.*

car·di·op·a·thy /kär dē ˈo pə thē/ n. a disease or disorder of the heart. *Can a healthy diet and routine exercise prevent cardiopathy?*

ca·su·al /ˈka zhə wəl/ adj. relaxed; informal. *Kevin played a casual game of beach volleyball yesterday.*

cat·e·go·ries /ˈka tə gôr ēz/ n. pl. plural of CATEGORY; divisions within a system; classifications. *How many categories are in archery competitions?*

cel·e·brate /ˈse lə brāt/ v. to commemorate a notable occasion with festivities. *Donavan will celebrate the victory with his teammates.*

cel·lu·loid /ˈsel yə loid/ n. **1** a transparent, plastic material. *A table-tennis ball is made of white or orange celluloid.* adj. **2** having the qualities of a transparent, plastic material. *The celluloid ball was hollow and very light.*

bungalow

cen·trif·u·gal /sen 'tri fyə gəl/ *adj.* directed away from a center. *Centrifugal force is required to throw a discus.*

cer·tain·ly /'sûr tən lē/ *adv.* definitely. *Know certainly that the Lord, our God, hears our prayers.*

chal·leng·ing /'cha lən jing/ *adj.* presenting a challenge; difficult. *Surfing was an extremely challenging assignment.*

cham·pi·ons /'cham pē ənz/ *n. pl.* plural of CHAMPION; more than one champion; winners. *The champions received gold medals.*

cham·pi·on·ship /'cham pē ən ship/ *n.* a contest to determine a champion. *The best football team won the championship.*

chan·de·lier /shan də 'lîr/ *n.* derived from FRENCH; a decorative lighting fixture with multiple bulbs or candles, hung from a ceiling. *A crystal chandelier hung in the grand ballroom.*

chan·nel /'cha nəl/ *n.* a specific band of frequencies that broadcast a television or radio program. *Uncle Ted and I watched the World Series on the sports channel.*

char·i·ty /'châr ə tē/ *n.* impartial, Christian love. *The Lord wants us to have fervent charity toward each other.*

chauf·feur /shō 'fûr/ *n.* derived from FRENCH; a hired driver. *The chauffeur drove the heiress to her riding lessons.*

chlo·rine /'klôr ēn/ *n.* a chemical used for water purification. *Can you smell the chlorine in a swimming pool?*

chop·sticks /'chop stiks/ *n. pl.* derived from CHINESE; plural of CHOPSTICK; two sticks used to pick up food. *Jung dropped the chopsticks on the table.*

chow mein /'chou mān/ *n.* derived from CHINESE; a seasoned stew of meat and vegetables served with fried noodles. *Chow mein is a simple dish to make.*

cir·cuit /'sûr kət/ *n.* a circular course or path. *Chad maintained good form as he followed the challenging circuit.*

cir·cum·spect·ly /'sûr kəm spekt lē/ *adv.* carefully examining each possibility; prudently. *Judges at the horse show surveyed the field circumspectly.*

cir·cum·stan·ces /'sûr kəm stant səz/ *n. pl.* plural of CIRCUMSTANCE; conditions or events surrounding a particular situation; the way something happens. *Do you know the circumstances of the game cancellation?*

cir·cum·vent /sûr kəm 'vent/ *v.* to manage to go around; to avoid. *Hugh tried to circumvent the obstacle by reining in his horse.*

clar·i·ty /'klâr ə tē/ *n.* a state of being clear; lucidness. *Concentration and clarity of mind are vital when competing.*

close·ly /'klōs lē/ *adv.* in close proximity. *Each of the BMX riders followed closely behind the other.*

col·le·giate /kə 'lē jət/ *adj.* relating to college. *Players in the collegiate conference are university students.*

col·lide /kə 'līd/ *v.* to crash. *Offensive and defensive players often collide.*

col·li·sions /kə 'li zhənz/ *n. pl.* plural of COLLISION; crashes. *Collisions between players are common in hockey.*

com·mit·tee /kə 'mi tē/ *n.* a group convened for a specific purpose and goal. *The committee will seek land to build a new stadium.*

com·mon sense /'ko mən sents/ *n.* good judgment. *One should use common sense when playing in or around water.*

com·mu·ni·ty /kə 'myoō nə tē/ *n.* neighborhood. *Our community has an indoor football stadium.*

com·mu·ni·ty cen·ter /kə 'myoo nə tē sen tûr/ *n.* a building used for community activities. *During renovations, the team used the pool at the community center.*

¹**com·pact** /kəm 'pakt/ *v.* combine; to press together. *Michaella began to compact the swim gear into her bag.*

²**com·pact** /kom 'pakt/ *adj.* occupying a small space. *The swim team could not fit into the coach's compact car.*

com·pan·ion /kəm 'pan yən/ *n.* one who shares in what the other is doing; friend. *Jesus is our ever faithful and loyal companion.*

com·pe·ten·cy /'kom pə tənt sē/ *n.* an adequate ability to perform a task. *Students must demonstrate competency to receive a black belt.*

com·pe·ti·tion /kom pə 'ti shən/ *n.* a contest between opponents. *The waterskiing competition was held on Lake Powell.*

com·pet·i·tive /kəm 'pe tə tiv/ *adj.* desiring to compete; aggressive. *Competitive athletes enjoy the thrill of a competition.*

com·ple·ment /'kom plə mənt/ *v.* to fill up, complete, or perfect something else. *Judd's skills complement the swim team.*

com·pli·ment /'kom plə mənt/ *n.* an expression of admiration or praise. *Rae received a compliment from Bonnie for her improved time.*

com·pos·ite /kom 'po zət/ *adj.* made up of different parts; combination. *Skateboard decks made of wood are preferred over composite ones.*

com·po·si·tion /kom pə 'zi shən/ *n.* a state of thoroughly placing together; construction of. *Did Derrell write a composition about the rules of table tennis?*

con·ceit /kən 'sēt/ *n.* too high an opinion of oneself or of one's ability to do things; egotism. *Bragging about one's own abilities shows conceit.*

con·cen·tra·tion /kont sən 'trā shən/ *n.* the direction of focused attention to a particular task; thought. *Ann was in deep concentration during the table-tennis game.*

con·cen·tric /kən 'sen trik/ *adj.* having a common center or midpoint; circular shaped. *The bull's eye is in the middle of concentric circles.*

con·cerned /kən 'sûrnd/ *v.* past tense of CONCERN; to be thoroughly anxious about a certain situation; worried. *Chelsea was concerned about the weather during the long-jump event.*

con·ces·sions /kən 'se shənz/ *n. pl.* plural of CONCESSION; smaller businesses on the premises of larger businesses. *Hal visited the concessions to get some snacks during the game.*

con·cludes /kən 'kloodz/ *v.* ends. *When the game concludes, we will celebrate.*

con·dense /kən 'dents/ *v.* to make more compact. *I will try to condense my narrative into a few paragraphs.*

con·di·tion·ing /kən 'di shə ning/ *n.* a training process. *The conditioning of muscles assists in one's overall performance.*

con·fi·dent /'kon fə dənt/ *adj.* certain. *The boys are confident they will be able to go kayaking in June.*

con·fig·ured /kən 'fi gyûrd/ *v.* past tense of CONFIGURE; set up in a particular way. *The coach configured the plays on a chalkboard.*

con·fined /kən 'find/ *v.* past tense of CONFINE; to have thoroughly kept within a boundary. *Is the race confined to the area north or south of the bridge?*

confinement   **corporate**

con·fine·ment /kən ˈfin mənt/ *n.* that which is being thoroughly kept within a boundary. *There is an area in the marina for the confinement of the boats.*

con·grat·u·la·tions /kən gra chə ˈlā shənz/ *n. pl.* plural of CONGRATULATION; expressions of praise, good wishes, or compliments. *Numerous fans expressed their congratulations after the golf game.*

con·i·cal /ˈko ni kəl/ *adj.* having the shape of a cone; cone shaped. *Shuttlecocks, used in badminton, are conical in shape.*

con·sci·en·tious /kont shē ˈent shəs/ *adj.* meticulous; thorough; careful. *Jacques was conscientious as he focused on the putting green.*

con·stant /ˈkont stənt/ *adj.* faithfulness; consistent. *The constant love of our Savior is unending.*

con·struc·tion /kən ˈstruk shən/ *n.* the process of building something. *Will is using wood for the construction of the canoe.*

con·tact /ˈkon takt/ *n.* a state of interaction. *Alisa came into contact with many professional racers at Supercross.*

con·tend·ers /kən ˈten dûrz/ *n. pl.* plural of CONTENDER; competitors or contestants. *There are many contenders in the competitive sport of table tennis.*

¹con·tent /kən ˈtent/ *adj.* satisfied. *Wade did his best at the meet, so he is content with his diving score.*

²con·tent /ˈkon tent/ *n.* something contained. *The content of your character depicts your attitude and personality.*

con·tes·tants /kən ˈtes tənts/ *n. pl.* plural of CONTESTANT; competitors; participants. *Brock was among the fifty long-jump contestants at the meet.*

con·tin·u·ous /kən ˈtin yoō əs/ *adj.* having the quality of continuing. *Olympic athletes participate in continuous training sessions.*

¹con·trast /ˈkon trast/ *n.* a sharp or striking difference. *The contrast of colors on the swimsuits was striking.*

²con·trast /kən ˈtrast/ *v.* to compare the differences of. *Can you contrast synchronized swimmers and competitive swimmers?*

con·vince /kən ˈvints/ *v.* to persuade. *Can you convince your friends to rent a motorboat?*

co·op·er·ate /kō ˈo pə rāt/ *v.* to collaborate. *BMX riders need to cooperate with each other.*

co·op·er·a·tion /kō o pə ˈrā shən/ *n.* the act of working together to achieve a common goal; collaboration or compliance. *Team cooperation is necessary for a successful outcome.*

co·or·di·na·tion /kō ôr də ˈnā shən/ *n.* the skillful movement of parts for effective results; dexterity. *The game of table tennis requires a lot of coordination.*

cor·dial /ˈkôr jəl/ *adj.* sincere; friendly. *Gabe gave a cordial smile to his new teammate.*

cor·po·rate /ˈkôr pə rət/ *adj.* to act as one unified body of individuals. *It was a corporate decision to donate funds for the new athletic club.*

construction

cor·po·ra·tion /kôr pə 'rā shən/ *n.* the state of a group of individuals acting as one unified body. *The new racquetball corporation was headed by Ed and Gigi.*

coun·cil /'kount səl/ *n.* a club; a group that makes rules and takes care of other matters for a larger group. *The swim council meets every Tuesday.*

coun·sel /'kount səl/ *v.* **1** to advise. *A good coach will counsel athletes to help improve their skills.* *n.* **2** advice. *My coach's counsel helped me improve my breathing technique.*

coun·ter·clock·wise /koun tûr 'klok wīz/ *adv.* the circular direction that is opposite of the way the hands on a clock move. *Track-and-field races are run counterclockwise.*

cou·ple /'ku pəl/ *v.* to fasten, link, or join. *Selena will couple her boots to her skis before riding the ski lift.*

cou·ra·geous /kə 'rā jəs/ *adj.* having the quality of courage. *Despite injuries, the courageous athlete kept going.*

crouch·ing /'krou ching/ *n.* **1** the lowering of one's body position by bending the legs. *The runners began by crouching in the starting blocks.* *v.* **2** lowering one's body by bending the legs. *Karl was crouching in readiness for the start of the race.*

cru·cial /'kroō shəl/ *adj.* very important; essential. *Faith in Jesus is crucial for salvation.*

cul·tur·al /'kul chə rəl/ *adj.* relating to a culture. *Table tennis is a popular, cultural sport in Asia.*

cush·ioned /'koo shənd/ *v.* **1** past tense of CUSHION; to have protected against impact. *Foam mats cushioned Malik's fall after his pole-vault attempt.* *adj.* **2** soft. *The cushioned, landing pad was very plush.*

cus·tom·ar·y /'kus tə mâr ē/ *adj.* usual; common. *Matches of odd numbers are customary in tournament table tennis.*

cy·cling /'sī kə ling/ *n.* shortened form of BICYCLING. *Is BMX cycling an Olympic sport?*

D

dan·ger·ous /'dān jə rəs/ *adj.* hazardous; unsafe. *The sport of motocross racing is very dangerous.*

day·dream /'dā drēm/ *n.* a pleasant waking thought. *Alana was lost in a daydream about a bike race.*

dec·la·ra·tion /de klə 'rā shən/ *n.* the state of making your position thoroughly clear; an announcement. *The judge made a declaration that unfair play results in elimination.*

de·coy /'dē koi/ *n.* someone or something used to divert the attention of another person. *The decoy was used to help the climber to not be fearful.*

de·fense /'dē fents/ *n.* the sports team members who defend and carry out methods to prevent the other team from scoring. *Celeste played on defense during the last four games.*

cycling

definitely

def·i·nite·ly /'de fə nit lē/ *adv.* certainly; clearly; without a doubt. *Chrissy definitely had the advantage in the last golf tournament.*

de·flect /di 'flekt/ *v.* to bend away from a fixed direction. *Sunglasses deflect light rays from a rider's eyes.*

de·hy·dra·tion /dē hī 'drā shən/ *n.* a depletion of body fluids. *Dehydration from lack of fluids in the body is very dangerous.*

del·i·ca·tes·sen /de li kə 'te sən/ *n.* derived from GERMAN; a store where ready-to-eat food products are sold. *After archery practice, our family ate lunch at a delicatessen.*

de·part·ed /di 'pär təd/ *v.* past tense of DEPART; to have left or proceeded. *The bus departed from the stadium after the competition.*

de·scrib·ing /di 'skrī bing/ *v.* giving a thorough account. *Matthias wrote a story describing his rock-climbing adventure.*

de·scrip·tion /di 'skrip shən/ *n.* the state or process of explanation; an explanation. *The announcer gave a detailed description of the game's highlights.*

de·signed /di 'zīnd/ *v.* past tense of DESIGN; to have planned. *The BMX bike was designed with smaller wheels than other bikes.*

de·signs /di 'zīnz/ *n. pl.* plural of DESIGN; something's structure and form; models. *Regan submitted her snowboard designs into the competition.*

de·tec·tion /di 'tek shən/ *n.* the state of thoroughly uncovering the facts. *In fencing, a machine scores the detection of a touch to an opponent.*

deuce /'do͞os/ *n.* a tie at 40 in tennis that requires two consecutive points by one side to win. *Shelby finally won the tennis game after the deuce with Ian.*

dignity

de·vel·op·ment /di 've ləp mənt/ *n.* a result of planning. *An improvement to the equipment was a positive development.*

dex·ter·i·ty /dek 'stâr ə tē/ *n.* physical and mental skill. *Martin's dexterity in fencing is remarkable.*

di·ag·o·nal·ly /dī 'a gə nə lē/ *adv.* in a diagonal manner. *When Edwin served the ball, it went diagonally into the service box.*

di·a·gram /'dī ə gram/ *n.* a drawing that shows relations of parts. *Coach Sid drew a diagram of the new play strategy.*

di·a·lect /'dī ə lekt/ *n.* a type of language spoken across a specific area or region. *Joyce spoke the Cantonese dialect fluently during her visit to China.*

di·am·e·ter /dī 'a mə tûr/ *n.* a line segment passing through the center of a circle having end points on the circle. *A circle's diameter passes through its midpoint.*

die·sel /'dē zəl/ *n.* derived from GERMAN; a vehicle with a diesel engine. *Uncle Delmar drove his diesel to the archery tournament.*

di·e·tar·y /'dī ə târ ē/ *adj.* related to diet. *Athletes often follow their coaches' dietary advice.*

dif·fi·cult /'di fi kəlt/ *adj.* complex; complicated. *Carrie maneuvered through the difficult course on her motorcycle.*

dif·fi·cul·ty /'di fi kəl tē/ *n.* not easy to achieve. *Each dive is assigned a level of difficulty.*

dig·ni·fy /'dig nə fī/ *v.* to make worthy of; to honor, distinguish, or give distinction. *Golf does dignify the character of many people who play the game.*

dig·ni·ty /'dig nə tē/ *n.* a state of being worthy; self-respect. *Arturo had dignity and did not cheat while writing his golf score.*

di·lem·ma /də 'le mə/ *n.* an unwanted choice. *Karishma faced a dilemma with courage.*

dil·i·gence /'di lə jənts/ *n.* perseverance in performing one's obligations. *It is important to study God's Word with diligence.*

di·men·sions /də 'ment shənz/ *n. pl.* plural of DIMENSION; measurements. *What are the dimensions of your long board?*

dis·a·bil·i·ty /dis ə 'bi lə tē/ *n.* the condition of not being completely able-bodied. *An athlete with a disability ran in the Paralympics.*

dis·be·lief /dis bə 'lēf/ *n.* mental rejection as if untrue; incredulous. *Joe was in disbelief when he qualified for the competition.*

dis·cern·ment /di 'sûrn mənt/ *n.* that which shows distinguished judgment, perception, or sensitivity. *Darby used discernment as she gauged her long-jump approach.*

dis·ci·plined /'di sə plənd/ *v.* **1** past tense of DISCIPLINE; to have exercised self-control; to have made oneself do something regularly. *Stella disciplined herself to run fifteen miles a week.* *adj.* **2** self-controlled. *Disciplined athletes have regular workouts.*

dis·cus·sion /di 'sku shən/ *n.* an oral consideration of a question or idea. *Was there a discussion held about wheelchair basketball?*

dis·grace /dis 'grās/ *v.* not pleasing others; to bring shame. *Soon-Yee did not want to disgrace her family by behaving badly.*

dis·guise /dis 'gīz/ *v.* to conceal. *Dave could not disguise his disappointment after losing the match.*

dis·heart·ened /dis 'här tənd/ *adj.* discouraged; dismayed. *Coach Judy told the team to not be disheartened after losing the meet.*

dis·lo·ca·tion /dis lō 'kā shən/ *n.* a separation of a bone at a joint. *DeVon ran the race even with a dislocation to one of his fingers.*

dis·po·si·tion /dis pə 'zi shən/ *n.* a state of certain behavior when placed under specific circumstances; personality. *Gwen had a cheerful disposition during the tournament.*

dis·re·spect·ful /dis ri 'spekt fəl/ *adj.* not showing proper honor. *Todd did not want to appear disrespectful and interrupt a game.*

dis·rup·tion /dis 'rup shən/ *n.* the state of breaking something apart or interrupting. *A flash of lightning was a disruption to the event at the meet.*

dis·solve /di 'zolv/ *v.* to loosen or melt apart. *The added pool chemicals should dissolve after a few minutes.*

dis·tinc·tion /di 'stingk shən/ *n.* the state of standing out from others. *Kareema had the distinction of being the tallest player on the team.*

dis·tinc·tive /di 'stingk tiv/ *adj.* standing out from others. *A distinctive feature of kendo is the use of bamboo sticks as swords.*

div·ot /'di vət/ *n.* a loose lump of grass and dirt that is dug out of the ground during a sport such as golf. *Emmi replaced each divot after teeing off in her golf game.*

do·mes·ti·cat·ed /də 'mes ti kā təd/ *adj.* adapted to live in association with humans; tamed. *Horses were domesticated centuries ago.*

dom·i·nate /'do mə nāt/ *v.* to be the master over something or someone. *The Eagles sought to dominate the competition.*

dominating

dom·i·nat·ing /ˈdo mə nā ting/ v. mastering, controlling, or having power over others. *Gloria was dominating the racquetball court and winning.*

dom·i·neer·ing /do mə ˈnîr ing/ adj. bossy. *Brady's parents were worried about his domineering attitude.*

do·min·ion /də ˈmi nyən/ n. the state of supreme authority. *Jesus has dominion over all the earth.*

dor·mant /ˈdôr mənt/ adj. the state of being asleep; inactive. *The flowers that had been dormant began to bloom.*

dor·mi·to·ry /ˈdôr mə tôr ē/ n. a place to go to sleep; a residence hall usually without private bathrooms. *The boys slept in a dormitory during sports camp.*

dos·age /ˈdō sij/ n. the frequency and amount of the dispensation of a drug. *The team doctor recommended a dosage of aspirin for pain relief.*

down·pour /ˈdoun pôr/ n. a heavy, sustained shower of rain. *The sudden downpour drenched the field and caused a long delay.*

dres·sage /drə ˈsäzh/ n. the precise movements of a thoroughly trained horse; horsemanship. *Marie trains horses in dressage.*

drought /ˈdrout/ n. a long period of dry weather. *Falling snow was a welcome sight after the period of drought.*

du·ra·tion /doo ˈrā shən/ n. the state of or the period of time for which something lasts. *Reporters waited for the duration of the marathon to see the winner.*

E

ec·lec·tic /e ˈklek tik/ adj. related to a gathering of various sources; diverse. *There was an eclectic selection of ski equipment at the store.*

embraced

e·del·weiss /ˈā dəl vīs/ n. derived from GERMAN; a flower with woolly leaves native to central or southeast Europe. *An edelweiss grows in high altitudes above the tree line.*

el·e·vat·ed /ˈe lə vā təd/ v. past tense of ELEVATE; to have raised, lifted, or advanced. *The high-jump crossbar was elevated to a record height.*

e·lim·i·na·tion /i li mə ˈnā shən/ n. removal; exclusion. *Helen's elimination from the meet was due to illness.*

e·lon·gate /i ˈlông gāt/ v. to make longer; lengthen. *Runners will elongate their stride to cover more ground.*

el·o·quent /ˈe lə kwənt/ adj. expressive. *Coach's halftime speech was not eloquent, but it was effective.*

em·bar·rassed /im ˈbâr əsd/ v. past tense of EMBARRASS; humiliated; to have caused an uneasy feeling. *Old stories about Bart's beginning attempts at golf embarrassed him.*

em·bod·ied /im ˈbo dēd/ v. past tense of EMBODY; to be in bodily form; personified. *Dana embodied all the qualities of a fine Christian athlete.*

em·braced /im ˈbrāsd/ v. past tense of EMBRACE; placed into one's arms. *Luis' father embraced him when he completed his first race.*

downpour

em·pha·size /ˈemp fə sīz/ *v.* to place an importance on something; stress. *Smart hockey parents emphasize the fun of the game.*

en·chi·la·da /en chə ˈlä də/ *n.* derived from SPANISH; a tortilla wrapped around a mixture, covered with chili sauce, and baked. *The enchilada that Aunt Rosa served was warm and delicious.*

en·coun·ter /in ˈkoun tûr/ *v.* coming up against something unexpectedly. *A snowboarder should be ready to encounter numerous hazards.*

en·dur·ance /in ˈdoor ənts/ *n.* the ability to tolerate prolonged exertion or activity; stamina. *Volleyball players need to have a lot of endurance.*

en·dur·ing /in ˈdoor ing/ *v.* to last without quitting. *Kiley is enduring the training to be in a cross-country race.*

en·er·gi·zing /ˈe nûr ji zing/ *adj.* invigorating. *A quick game of badminton will be energizing.*

en·gine /ˈen jən/ *n.* a machine for powering equipment. *Jake's motorcycle has a modified and powerful engine.*

en·ter·tain·ment /en tûr ˈtān mənt/ *n.* **1** enjoyment; recreation. *Laney watched her brother's long-jump attempts for entertainment.* **2** performance; production. *Kent enjoyed the opening ceremony entertainment before the final meet.*

e·ques·tri·an /i ˈkwes trē ən/ *adj.* relating to horsemanship. *Steeplechase and harness racing are both equestrian sports.*

e·qui·lib·ri·um /ē kwə ˈli brē əm/ *n.* a state of being in balance; balance. *Surfers can maintain their equilibrium during a long ride.*

e·quip·ment /i ˈkwip mənt/ *n.* the apparatus used in an activity or operation. *Motocross racers wear safety equipment such as body armor and boots.*

er·rant /ˈâr ənt/ *adj.* inclined to wander. *An errant climber greeted Ty when he reached the summit.*

er·ror /ˈâr ûr/ *n.* state of straying from what is correct. *Drew was very careful and did not make an error.*

es·pe·cial·ly /is ˈpesh lē/ *adv.* particularly. *It is especially important to practice free throws.*

es·sen·tial /i ˈsent shəl/ *adj.* absolutely necessary. *It is essential to warm up before practice.*

eth·nic·i·ty /eth ˈni sə tē/ *n.* background; ethnic origin. *Malia shared that her ethnicity was Asian-American.*

et·i·quette /ˈe ti kət/ *n.* derived from FRENCH; proper manners. *It is good etiquette for a rider to signal he is ready to begin.*

eu·phor·ic /yo͞o ˈfôr ik/ *adj.* extremely happy; overjoyed. *The team was euphoric after reaching the summit of the rock.*

ex·cel·lence /ˈek sə lənts/ *n.* superiority. *To glorify God in all we do, we should strive for excellence.*

engine

exception

ex·cep·tion /ik 'sep shən/ *n.* something excluded. *No exception will be made for anyone arriving late.*

ex·cla·ma·tion /eks klə 'mā shən/ *n.* a sharp utterance; a cry. *Shay voiced an exclamation when her name was called.*

ex·haust·ed /ig 'zȯ stəd/ *adj.* extremely tired. *Our Lord is always ready to help us and is never exhausted.*

ex·hi·bi·tion /ek sə 'bi shən/ *n.* **1** a display; a show. *The exhibition by horses with beautiful gaits intrigued Aimee.* *adj.* **2** related to a display or show. *The exhibition hall on Fairfield Street was used for the annual charity horse show.*

ex·panse /ik 'spants/ *n.* something spread out over an extensive distance. *The entire midfield expanse was dedicated to throwing events.*

ex·pel /ik 'spel/ *v.* to push or force out. *Yuri did expel a loud breath when the rubber ball hit him.*

ex·pe·ri·ence /ik 'spîr ē ənts/ *n.* direct observation and participation. *Robin learned better ways to ski through experience.*

ex·plo·sion /ik 'splō zhən/ *n.* a sudden, powerful burst. *A basket was accompanied by an explosion of applause.*

ex·po·si·tion /ek spə 'zi shən/ *n.* the state of placing items out in the view of the public; a fair or exhibition. *The archery team demonstrated their skills at the county exposition.*

ex·po·sure /ik 'spō zhur/ *n.* the process of being made known. *Soccer players receive a lot of exposure due to the sport's popularity.*

finalist

ex·tra·or·di·nar·y /ik 'strȯr də nâr ē/ *adj.* remarkable; unusual. *Erich completed an extraordinary feat when he ski jumped 400 feet!*

fa·cil·i·tate /fə 'si lə tāt/ *v.* assist with; aid. *Mel will facilitate the freestyle skiing competition as a judge.*

fa·mil·iar /fə 'mil yûr/ *adj.* well-known; easily recognized. *A spike is a familiar offensive technique in volleyball.*

fas·ten·ers /'fa sən ûrz/ *n. pl.* plural of FASTENER; connective devices. *Felix secured the fasteners on his boot before riding the half-pipe.*

fa·tigue /fə 'tēg/ *n.* weariness from exertion. *Mona collapsed with fatigue at the end of the race.*

feint /'fānt/ *n.* a mock attack to distract from what was really intended; a trick. *By using a feint, I was able to score the winning point.*

fi·ber·glass /'fī bûr glas/ *n.* a combination of glass fibers and plastic. *Pole vaulters use poles that are made of fiberglass.*

fi·es·ta /fē 'es tə/ *n.* derived from SPANISH; a festival. *My fencing club celebrated Cinco de Mayo with a fiesta.*

fi·nal /'fī nəl/ *adj.* related to an ending competition. *Lauren qualified for the final Pro Motocross event.*

fi·na·le /fə 'na lē/ *n.* derived from ITALIAN; the final portion of a performance. *The gaited Paso Fino performed the finale of the horse show.*

fi·nal·ist /'fī nə list/ *n.* one who is qualified for an ending competition. *Curtis was a finalist in the Motocross World Championship.*

finalists

fi·nal·ists /ˈfi nə lists/ *n. pl.* plural of FINALIST; contestants who are qualified for an ending competition. *Abe and Cristiano were finalists in the World Championship match.*

fi·nal·ly /ˈfi nəl ē/ *adv.* related to the end of a series or process; at last. *After an extensive delay, the water-polo meet finally began.*

fis·sures /ˈfi shûrz/ *n. pl.* plural of FISSURE; long narrow cracks or openings; crevices. *Climbers often put their hands into fissures when climbing.*

flex·i·bil·i·ty /flek sə ˈbi lə tē/ *n.* the capability of bending easily; elasticity. *Experienced skaters have flexibility to perform stunts.*

flex·i·ble /ˈflek sə bəl/ *adj.* able to be bent; adaptable. *Kelly remained flexible about the idea of learning to surf.*

flex·ion /ˈflek shən/ *n.* a bending. *The flexion of the pole used for pole vaulting is very important.*

fo·cused /ˈfō kəsd/ *v.* past tense of FOCUS; to have concentrated thoughts. *Was Eliza focused during the long-jump training sessions?*

foot·work /ˈfoot wûrk/ *n.* skillful movement or maneuvering. *Quinn had quick footwork during the racquetball game.*

for·eign·er /ˈfôr ə nûr/ *n.* a person from or of another country than one's own; outsider. *A foreigner was a spectator at an international skating competition.*

for·ma·tions /fôr ˈmā shənz/ *n. pl.* plural of FORMATION; shapes or patterns. *Yosemite National Park is known for its beautiful rock formations.*

for·mi·da·ble /fôr ˈmi də bəl/ *adj.* remarkable; impressive. *Aaron showed formidable skills with his new long-jump record.*

generation

frame·work /ˈfrām wûrk/ *n.* a skeletal structure. *The framework for the new boat is almost finished.*

frank·furt·er /ˈfrangk fûr tûr/ *n.* derived from GERMAN; a cured, cooked sausage that is either skinless or stuffed in a casing. *Corinne ordered a frankfurter when her team went out to eat.*

free·style /ˈfrē stī əl/ *adj.* with free choice of style. *Britt competed in the freestyle, half-pipe event.*

fre·quent /ˈfrē kwənt/ *adj.* happening often. *The Fry family takes frequent trips to the river to go kayaking.*

func·tion /ˈfungk shən/ *n.* a purpose, action, or role. *What is the function of large wheels on a race motorcycle?*

func·tion·al /ˈfungk shə nəl/ *adj.* the state of performing. *The powerboat's engine was functional.*

fu·ton /ˈfoō ton/ *n.* derived from JAPANESE; a cotton mattress often used with a frame. *We use a futon as a bed for our guests.*

ga·ra·ges /gə ˈrä jəz/ *n. pl.* plural of GARAGE; buildings for parking, storing, or repairing vehicles. *John took his car to three different garages for repair quotes.*

gauge /ˈgāj/ *v.* to estimate or judge. *A good competitor can gauge his opponent's next move.*

gen·er·a·tion /je nə ˈrā shən/ *n.* **1** the state of time between the birth of parents and their offspring. *Each generation must teach others about the good news of Jesus.* **2** a group of people born at approximately the same time. *Hillary was interested in researching the history of her grandparent's generation.*

ge·sund·heit /gə 'zoont hīt/ *interj.* derived from GERMAN; a polite comment to wish someone good health after he or she has sneezed. *After I sneezed, Delaney said, "Gesundheit!"*

goal·keep·er /'gōl kē pûr/ *n.* a player who defends a goal in a sport. *The goalkeeper dove and successfully blocked the kick.*

gog·gles /'go gəlz/ *n.* protective glasses in a plastic or rubber frame that fits snugly against the face to protect the eyes. *Do you wear goggles when you swim?*

gour·met /goor 'mā/ *adj.* derived from FRENCH; relating to a refined taste in food. *Gourmet cheeses were served at the riding academy's open house.*

gra·cious /'grā shəs/ *adj.* marked by pleasantness and courtesy. *The sixth grade class is known for its gracious behavior.*

gra·di·ent /'grā dē ənt/ *n.* a slope. *Grandpa walked down the short gradient to get into the kayak.*

grad·u·al·ly /'gra jə wə lē/ *adv.* slowly; steadily. *Kari noticed that the day was gradually getting warmer.*

graph·ite /'gra fīt/ *n.* a composite material in which carbon fibers are the reinforcing material. *Dena bought a bow made of graphite at the sporting goods store.*

grate·ful /'grāt fəl/ *adj.* full of thanks; thankful. *I am grateful that God forgives me of my sins.*

grat·i·fy /'gra tə fī/ *v.* to do something that makes someone pleased. *Does it gratify you that the Lord provides for our needs?*

grief /'grēf/ *n.* deep sadness caused by trouble or loss; sorrow. *The team experienced grief when it was disqualified last year.*

gui·tar /gə 'tär/ *n.* derived from SPANISH; a stringed musical instrument. *Greg enjoys playing the guitar and singing praises to the Lord.*

gung ho /'gung hō/ *adj.* derived from CHINESE; overly enthusiastic. *When we learned of a Bible study, we were gung ho to get started.*

gym·na·si·um /jim 'nā zē əm/ *n.* a large, exercise room. *The college volleyball match was held in the gymnasium.*

ham·burg·er /'ham bûr gûr/ *n.* derived from GERMAN; ground beef; a sandwich consisting of a ground beef patty on a round bun. *Kurt likes to eat his hamburger with mustard and ketchup.*

hand·ling /'hand ling/ *v.* touching; managing. *Goalkeepers may use two hands when handling the ball in water polo.*

haz·ards /'ha zûrdz/ *n. pl.* plural of HAZARD; obstacles on a golf course, such as a lake or sand trap, that are either naturally or artificially constructed. *The newly designed golf course contained many water hazards.*

goalkeeper

height

height /ˈhīt/ *n.* the distance from top to bottom of someone or something standing upright. *Because of her height, Nicole played center.*

hel·met /ˈhel mət/ *n.* protective headgear. *It is important to wear a sturdy helmet when riding a bike.*

her·o·ism /ˈhîr ə wi zəm/ *n.* the act of being a hero. *I admire the heroism of athletes who have spoken out for Christ.*

hic·cup /ˈhi kəp/ *v.* **1** to make an involuntary gulp. *Simon heard Matt hiccup after the championship Grand Prix.* *n.* **2** an involuntary gulp. *A loud hiccup came from Jeremy's mouth.*

high·lights /ˈhī līts/ *n. pl.* plural of HIGHLIGHT; featured items of interest. *One of the race highlights was a spectacular jump.*

hor·i·zon·tal /hôr ə ˈzon təl/ *adj.* relating to a plane parallel to the horizon. *The long jump measures one's ability to jump a horizontal distance.*

hurl·ing /ˈhûr ling/ *n.* throwing forward forcefully. *The gold medalist won by hurling the javelin over twenty meters.*

hy·brid /ˈhī brəd/ *adj.* something formed by merging two original designs. *Hybrid bikes are a cross between motorcycles and mountain bikes.*

hy·drop·a·thy /hī ˈdro pə thē/ *n.* a method of treating disease by the frequent use of water both internally and externally. *Hydropathy was a method to cure disease in the nineteenth century.*

hy·dro·pla·ning /ˈhī drə plā ning/ *n.* skimming across water. *Waterskiing involves hydroplaning over the surface of the water.*

hy·dro·scope /ˈhī drə skōp/ *n.* an instrument used for viewing objects deep below the surface of water. *Tyrone is a pipeline inspector who uses a hydroscope to detect leaks.*

immediately

hy·dro·ther·a·py /hī drə ˈthâr ə pē/ *adj.* the use of water for healing. *Hydrotherapy baths are often used to relieve headaches and stress.*

hy·dro·ther·mal /hī drə ˈthûr məl/ *adj.* relating to hot water. *A hydrothermal vent spewed water through a crack in the ocean floor.*

I

i·de·al·ly /ī ˈdē ə lē/ *adv.* optimally; perfectly. *Ideally, one should remove the kickstand on a BMX bike.*

i·den·ti·fi·ca·tion /ī den tə fə ˈkā shən/ *n.* evidence or proof of identity. *Different colored caps provide identification in water polo.*

il·lu·sion /i ˈloo zhən/ *n.* something that is not real. *The reflection of the sun on the water gave the illusion of fire.*

im·ag·i·nar·y /i ˈma jə nâr ē/ *adj.* related to the imagination. *I practiced with an imaginary discus before trying actual throws.*

im·i·tate /ˈi mə tāt/ *v.* copy. *Many children try to imitate the athletic style of their favorite athlete.*

im·me·di·ate·ly /i ˈmē dē ət lē/ *adv.* directly; at once; without delay. *Corrina immediately began to prepare for the pole-vault event.*

helmet

im·mi·grant /ˈi mə grənt/ *n.* one who has moved from one country to another. *Natasha was an immigrant from Russia.*

im·mov·a·ble /im ˈmo͞o və bəl/ *adj.* not able to be moved. *Immovable hurdles would be dangerous to runners.*

im·par·tial /im ˈpär shəl/ *adj.* free from bias; fair. *Judges at surfing competitions must be impartial.*

im·pose /im ˈpōz/ *v.* to put down, insist upon, or enforce. *Reina did impose her rules about penalties during the game.*

im·pos·si·bil·i·ty /im po sə ˈbi lə tē/ *n.* something not capable of happening. *J.J. thought it was an impossibility to jump over the high crossbar.*

im·prac·ti·cal /im ˈprak ti kəl/ *adj.* related to doing something that is not useful. *Heavy athletic wear is impractical during track-and-field competition.*

im·prove·ment /im ˈpro͞ov mənt/ *n.* the state of being improved; an advancement. *Allie made an improvement in her time in the 100-meter dash.*

im·pulse /ˈim pəls/ *n.* a sudden drive to act. *After the throwing events, Loni had an impulse to try the discus.*

in·com·pa·ra·ble /in ˈkom pə rə bəl/ *adj.* not able to be compared; unlike anything else. *Heaven's glory is incomparable to anything on the earth.*

in·cor·rupt·i·ble /in kə ˈrup tə bəl/ *adj.* not able to be ruined; not subject to corruption. *Our resurrected bodies will be incorruptible.*

in·cred·u·lous /in ˈkre jə ləs/ *adj.* not inclined to believe; unbelieving. *The coach was incredulous at his athletes' results.*

in·den·ta·tion /in den ˈtā shən/ *n.* a hollow or obvious depression. *The long-jump official measured the indentation in the sand.*

in·de·pen·dence /in də ˈpen dənts/ *n.* freedom. *Freestyle waterskiing provides independence from strict rules.*

in·de·scrib·a·ble /in di ˈskri bə bəl/ *adj.* not able to give a thorough account; indefinable. *The feeling of success in reaching the top was indescribable.*

in·di·vid·u·al /in də ˈvi jə wəl/ *n.* a person. *Each individual on a soccer team is responsible for his or her actions.*

in·ex·haust·i·ble /i nig ˈzȯ stə bəl/ *adj.* not able to be exhausted; tireless. *God's forgiveness and grace are inexhaustible.*

in·flec·tion /in ˈflek shən/ *n.* **1** the state of having a change in the pitch of one's voice. *I could tell by the inflection in her voice that she was excited.* **2** a suffix that changes the part of speech or function of a word. *The suffix -ed is an inflection that makes verbs past tense.*

in·flex·i·ble /in ˈflek sə bəl/ *adj.* not able to be bent; unbendable. *A good surfboard must be inflexible.*

in·frac·tion /in ˈfrak shən/ *n.* a violation; a failure to obey. *An infraction was called when Allison took the ball underwater.*

i·ni·ti·at·ed /i ˈni shē ā təd/ *v.* past tense of INITIATE; to have begun. *Jorge initiated the duel by moving his back foot.*

in·ju·ries /ˈin jə rēz/ *n. pl.* plural of INJURY; hurts or damages. *Hockey players wear protective gear to prevent injuries.*

in·no·cence /ˈi nə sənts/ *n.* state of causing no harm; blamelessness or guiltlessness. *The player in the penalty box kept protesting his innocence.*

in·no·cent·ly /ˈi nə sənt lē/ *adv.* not inclined to cause harm. *Randy innocently swept the puck into his own net.*

in·quire /in ˈkwī ûr/ *v.* to seek information. *Hank began to inquire about the new skate park hours.*

in·quir·y /in 'kwī ûr ē/ *n.* the state of seeking information; a request for information. *Ethan's inquiry helped him plan his weekend schedule.*

in·quis·i·tive /in 'kwi zə tiv/ *adj.* inclined to seek out knowledge; curious. *Rose was very inquisitive about the history of the pole vault.*

in·sist /in 'sist/ *v.* to take a stand and refuse to change; to persist and maintain. *The motorcycling federation does insist on strict safety measures.*

in·spec·tion /in 'spek shən/ *n.* state of looking into or closely observing. *A detailed inspection of ski equipment should be performed regularly.*

in·spec·tor /in 'spek tûr/ *n.* one who looks into matters. *An inspector checked the gymnasium floor before the match.*

in·spire /in 'spī ûr/ *v.* to have a positive influence in someone's life. *Does the life of the apostle Paul inspire you?*

in·spir·ing /in 'spī ûr ing/ *v.* having a continuously motivating influence on someone. *The faith of our forefathers is inspiring.*

in·sured /in 'shoord/ *adj.* to have obtained insurance for. *All players must be insured before they are allowed to play.*

in·sur·mount·a·ble /int sûr 'moun tə bəl/ *adj.* not able to be overcome; unconquerable. *Russ did not consider his disability to be insurmountable.*

in·tense /in 'tents/ *adj.* **1** to an extreme degree. *The motorboat was an intense shade of blue.* **2** showing great determination or zeal. *Vince's intense concentration showed on his face.*

in·ter·cep·tion /in tûr 'sep shən/ *n.* a pass intended for an offensive receiver that is caught by a defender. *A defender caught a pass for an interception.*

in·ter·fer·ence /in tûr 'fîr ənts/ *n.* interposing in a way that impedes a play. *A penalty was called for offensive interference.*

in·ter·mis·sion /in tûr 'mi shən/ *n.* a short break between the parts of an activity. *The surfing competition had a brief intermission at noon.*

in·ter·val /'in tûr vəl/ *n.* a period of time between two events. *Jocelyn rested during the interval and encouraged her teammates.*

in·tra·mu·ral /in trə 'myoor əl/ *adj.* occurring with the members of a single school. *Callie is the pitcher on her intramural softball team.*

in·tro·spec·tive /in trə 'spek tiv/ *adj.* inclined to examining one's own feelings; thoughtful. *Janeen shared her introspective viewpoint about the meet results.*

in·var·i·ab·ly /in 'vâr ē ə blē/ *adv.* not varying; always. *Derek practiced hard and invariably took first place.*

ir·re·triev·a·ble /ir i 'trē və bəl/ *adj.* incapable of recovering, regaining, or repairing. *The rubber ball was irretrievable after it bounced into the thick hedge.*

jour·nal·ism /'jûr nə li zəm/ *n.* the act of writing journals or periodicals. *Hope wanted to try journalism, so she wrote for the school paper.*

ka·ra·te /kə 'rä tē/ *n.* derived from JAPANESE; an unarmed martial art using kicks, punches, or blocks primarily for self-defense. *Valerie went to study karate at a dojo.*

kilograms

ki·lo·grams /ˈki lə gramz/ *n. pl.* plural of KILOGRAM; one thousand grams. *The men's discus weighs two kilograms.*

knowl·edge·a·ble /ˈno lij ə bəl/ *adj.* possessing a great deal of intelligence or awareness; wise. *Javier is knowledgeable about the rules of table tennis.*

kung fu /kəng ˈfoo/ *n.* derived from CHINESE; a martial art using open-handed techniques as well as weapons. *A wooden staff may be used for sparring in kung fu.*

L

lan·gua·ges /ˈlang gwi jəz/ *n. pl.* plural of LANGUAGE; the speech of races or nations; the means of expressing thoughts and feelings. *Sharon spoke four different languages by the age of twenty.*

laugh·ter /ˈlaf tûr/ *n.* the sound of laughing. *Laughter ensued when the winning goal was scored.*

league /ˈlēg/ *n.* a group of sports teams that play one another. *Keith's baseball team is in the south central league.*

lec·ture /ˈlek chûr/ *n.* a presentation of gathered information. *Malachi gave a lecture about table tennis to the university students.*

left-hand·ed /left ˈhan dəd/ *adj.* using the left hand. *Jeb is unique because he is the only left-handed player on the team.*

lei·sure /ˈlē zhûr/ *n.* free time not taken up with work or duties. *At his leisure, Grandpa watches professional skaters on television.*

lieu·ten·ant /loo ˈte nənt/ *n.* a person who acts in place of someone above him in authority; an officer. *The young lieutenant enjoys in-line skating during his free time.*

macrocosm

light·weight /ˈlīt wāt/ *adj.* having the quality of being light in weight. *Badminton rackets are lightweight.*

lin·e·ar /ˈli nē ûr/ *adj.* having the quality of a line; straight. *The winner had the longest discus throw in linear meters.*

lin·guis·tics /ling ˈgwis tiks/ *n.* related to the study of language. *Lester is proficient in the area of linguistics.*

li·ver·wurst /ˈli vûr wûrst/ *n.* derived from GERMAN; sausage made from ground liver that is spreadable. *Did you know that liverwurst is high in iron and vitamin A?*

lock·er room /ˈlo kûr room/ *n.* a room used by sports players to store equipment and change clothes. *The water-polo team prayed in the locker room before the big meet.*

M

mac·a·ro·ni /ma kə ˈrō nē/ *n.* derived from ITALIAN; a pasta that is shaped in the form of a tube. *Macaroni and cheese was available at the rodeo.*

ma·chin·er·y /mə ˈshē nə rē/ *n.* machines in general. *The machinery that resurfaces the ice in a rink is indispensible.*

mac·ro·cosm /ˈma krə ko zəm/ *n.* the universe. *God is the creator and ruler of the macrocosm, the universe.*

kung fu

mac·ro·scop·ic /ma krə 'sko pik/ *adj.* large enough to be seen without magnification. *Some algae are macroscopic.*

main·te·nance /'mān tə nənts/ *n.* upkeep of equipment or property. *Theresa was the head of lawn maintenance for the private club.*

maize /'māz/ *n.* derived from SPANISH; Indian corn. *Mamá Negrete bought maize at the store today.*

mal·func·tion /mal 'fungk shən/ *n.* **1** a state of performing badly; a breakdown. *The motorboat suffered an engine malfunction.* *v.* **2** to perform badly; to break down. *No sooner had the group left the dock than the engine began to malfunction.*

ma·neu·vers /mə 'noo vûrz/ *n. pl.* plural of MANEUVER; movement involving skill and expert physical movement; tricks. *Can you perform any maneuvers on in-line skates?*

ma·ri·a·chi /mär ē 'ä chē/ *adj.* derived from SPANISH; a Mexican street band. *While we ate at the Mexican restaurant, a mariachi band played.*

mea·sur·a·ble /'me zhə rə bəl/ *adj.* capable of being measured. *Extra training gave the team a measurable edge this season.*

mea·sure·ment /'me zhŭr mənt/ *n.* the dimension obtained by measuring. *The measurement of Andrea's throw in the shot put was ten meters.*

me·di·um /'mē dē əm/ *adj.* average; intermediate. *Cindi chose a track of medium length.*

med·ley /'med lē/ *n.* an assortment or mixture. *A medley relay consists of swimmers doing different strokes.*

meth·od /'me thəd/ *n.* an approach to doing something; an orderly system. *Sherri followed a specific training method when preparing to race.*

me·thod·i·cal /mə 'tho di kəl/ *adj.* following a method; thorough. *Excellence in martial arts requires methodical training.*

me·tic·u·lous /mə 'ti kyə ləs/ *adj.* conscientious; thorough; careful. *Margot was meticulous in the landscaping of the golf course.*

mi·cro·cosm /'mī krə ko zəm/ *n.* a diminished size or scale. *A drop of pond water may contain a microcosm of life.*

mi·cro·graph /'mī krə graf/ *adj.* a reproduction of an image of an object formed through a microscope. *Scientists use micrograph images to study viruses.*

mi·cro·phone /'mī krə fōn/ *n.* a device used to change sound waves into electrical impulses for the purpose of recording or amplifying the sounds. *The referee used a microphone to announce the badminton score.*

mi·cro·scop·ic /mī krə 'sko pik/ *adj.* too small to be seen without magnification under a microscope. *Many animal and plant cells are microscopic.*

mid·field /'mid fēld/ *n.* the middle of the field. *The medal ceremony was held in the midfield.*

maize

midsole

mid·sole /'mid sōl/ *n.* the middle part of a shoe's sole. *Some running shoes have a soft, supportive midsole.*

mi·grate /'mi grāt/ *v.* to move from one country to another. *Some hummingbirds migrate to Central America.*

mil·lion·aire /mil yə 'nâr/ *n.* a very wealthy person whose wealth is estimated at a million dollars, pounds, or another currency unit; tycoon. *An athlete can become a millionaire through product endorsements.*

min·i·a·ture /'mi nē ə choor/ *adj.* small; tiny. *Carlo bought a miniature version of golf clubs for his son, Ajay.*

mis·man·aged /mis 'ma nijd/ *v.* past tense of MISMANAGE; to have handled wrongly. *Sal mismanaged his money and could not pay the entrance fees.*

mis·treat·ed /mis 'trē təd/ *v.* past tense of MISTREAT; to have treated badly. *Shad mistreated his body by continuing to run with a stress fracture.*

mois·ture /'mois chŭr/ *n.* dampness; liquid spread out or concentrated in small drops. *Moisture on rocks can cause a climber to slip.*

mo·men·tous /mō 'men təs/ *adj.* important. *It was a momentous occasion when the Vipers defeated the Lions.*

mo·men·tum /mō 'men təm/ *n.* a force gained by motion. *Surfers use speed and momentum to ride up the face of a wave.*

mon·o·chro·mat·ic /mo nə krō 'ma tik/ *adj.* consisting of a single color or hue. *The team selected a monochromatic color scheme for uniforms.*

mon·o·gram /'mo nə gram/ *n.* a simple graphic formed by combining the initials in one's name. *Stuart has his monogram embroidered above his shirt pocket.*

nervous

mon·o·lith·ic /mo nə 'li thik/ *adj.* having the quality of being formed from a single stone block; huge in proportion. *Defeating the badminton champs seemed to be a monolithic task.*

mon·o·pod /'mo nə pod/ *n.* a one-legged support. *A tournament photographer used a monopod to support her camera.*

mo·to·cross /'mō tō kròs/ *n.* motorcycle cross-country racing. *The sport of motocross was the inspiration for BMX.*

mul·ti·cul·tur·al /məl ti 'kul chə rəl/ *adj.* many cultures. *The multicultural team included five nationalities.*

mul·ti·lane /'mul ti lān/ *adj.* a track with more than one lane. *The multilane track had staggered starting lines.*

mul·ti·lin·gual /məl tē 'ling gwəl/ *adj.* related to speaking several languages. *As a result of living in different countries, Meiko was multilingual.*

mul·ti·tal·ent·ed /məl ti 'ta lən təd/ *adj.* many abilities. *Gina is multitalented since she sings, paints, and runs well.*

mus·cu·lar /'mus kyə lŭr/ *adj.* relating to physical strength; brawny. *Playing hockey makes one quite muscular.*

N

nec·es·sar·y /'ne sə sâr ē/ *adj.* required; essential. *Diligent practice is necessary if one wants to improve in golf.*

ne·go·ti·ate /ni 'gō shē āt/ *v.* to travel successfully along; to navigate. *It can be difficult to negotiate around rocks while rafting.*

ner·vous /'nûr vəs/ *adj.* relating to the nerves; jumpy. *Even veteran competitors feel nervous before a track meet.*

neu·tral /ˈnoo trəl/ *adj.* without hue; lacking vivid color. *The colorful flowers surrounded the neutral hue of the rocks.*

news·wor·thy /ˈnooz wûr thē/ *adj.* interesting enough to warrant reporting to the public. *The blind man's ascent up the granite rock was a newsworthy event.*

notch /ˈnoch/ *n.* a V-shaped cut. *Sadie placed the notch at the end of the arrow into the bowstring.*

nour·ished /ˈnûr ishd/ *v.* past tense of NOURISH; sustained. *The healthy meal of protein nourished the athlete's body.*

nu·mer·i·cal /noo ˈmâr i kəl/ *adj.* relating to numbers. *Racers do not always line up in numerical order.*

ob·nox·ious /ob ˈnok shəs/ *adj.* rudely annoying. *The crowd's behavior during the game was obnoxious.*

ob·sta·cles /ˈob sti kəlz/ *n. pl.* plural of OBSTACLE; that which impedes the progress of something; barriers. *In barrel racing, horses need to turn quickly to avoid obstacles.*

ob·sti·nate /ˈob stə nət/ *adj.* resisting change; stubborn. *The obstinate player would not quit despite being injured.*

oc·ca·sion /ə ˈkā zhən/ *n.* an occurrence. *On one occasion, Jamie was tossed off her board by a huge wave.*

oc·cur·rence /ə ˈkûr ənts/ *n.* a happening; an event or incident. *An unexpected occurrence caused us to be late to the match.*

of·fense /ˈo fents/ *n.* the sports team members who attempt to score in a game. *Jerry led the offense to a victory in the final game.*

of·fi·cial /ə ˈfi shəl/ *n.* one whose duty is to act as a referee. *The official began the game with a jump ball.*

om·ni·scient /om ˈni shənt/ *adj.* all-knowing. *God is omniscient, omnipotent, and omnipresent.*

op·po·nents /ə ˈpō nənts/ *n. pl.* plural of OPPONENT; competitors. *The athletes were opponents on the court, but friends elsewhere.*

op·posed /ə ˈpōzd/ *v.* past tense of OPPOSE; to have been against something; was against. *Mitchell was opposed to drinking soda before working out.*

op·po·site /ˈo pə zət/ *adj.* something opposed or against another specified thing. *The teams lined up on opposite sides of the field.*

op·to·ki·net·ic /op tō kə ˈne tik/ *adj.* relating to the movement of the eyes. *Can an optometrist test the optokinetic ability of the eyes?*

op·tom·e·try /op ˈto mə trē/ *n.* the health care profession concerned with assisting patients to see clearly. *Kendall will study optometry to become an eye doctor.*

o·ri·gi·nal /ə ˈrij ə nəl/ *adj.* first; innovative; inventive. *Original table-tennis games were played on dining tables.*

out·crop·pings /ˈout kro pingz/ *n. pl.* plural of OUTCROPPING; parts of rock formations that jut out of the ground. *Sloan rested on one of the outcroppings along the trail.*

out·field·ers /ˈout fēl dûrz/ *n. pl.* plural of OUTFIELDER; the players in baseball or softball who play the defensive positions of left field, center field, and right field. *Two outfielders collided when they tried to catch the fly ball.*

P

pad·dling /ˈpad liŋ/ v. rowing with one's arms. *Alex was paddling out into the surf, hoping for a wave to break.*

pa·ja·mas /pə ˈjä məz/ n. pl. derived from HINDI; plural of PAJAMA; loose clothing worn for sleeping. *Tasvee wore her silk pajamas from India to bed.*

par·a·le·gal /pa rə ˈlē gəl/ n. a trained aide who assists a lawyer. *Sylvia spoke to the paralegal after her car accident.*

par·a·med·ic /pa rə ˈme dik/ n. a trained medical technician who performs emergency medical procedures in the absence of a doctor. *Bev wanted to be a paramedic and studied diligently.*

par·a·mount /ˈpär ə mount/ adj. greatest. *A true relationship with Jesus is a matter of paramount importance.*

par·a·pet /ˈpa rə pət/ n. derived from ITALIAN; a low wall or railing used as protection. *Avril's horse avoided the castle topped by the parapet.*

par·tic·i·pa·tion /pär ti sə ˈpā shən/ n. taking part in an activity. *Nathan's participation in martial arts has helped his balance.*

ped·es·tal /ˈpe dəs təl/ n. the supporting base of a column. *The team manager placed the trophy on the pedestal.*

pen·al·ties /ˈpe nəl tēz/ n. pl. plural of PENALTY; disadvantages imposed upon a person or team for a violation of the rules. *Numerous penalties caused the home team to lose.*

per·cent·age /pûr ˈsen tij/ n. a state of proportion within a group. *What percentage of high-jump athletes uses the Fosbury Flop method?*

¹per·mit /pûr ˈmit/ v. to allow; give consent; authorize. *The community pool director does not permit swimming alone.*

²per·mit /ˈpûr mit/ n. written permission; license. *Kelsi is excited to get her driver's permit.*

per·pen·dic·u·lar /pûr pən ˈdi kyə lûr/ adj. standing at right angles to a given plane or surface. *The water-skiers were perpendicular to the surface of the water.*

per·se·ver·ance /pûr sə ˈvîr ənts/ n. persistence; determination. *Trials in competition produce perseverance in Christ.*

per·spec·tive /pûr ˈspek tiv/ n. the inclination to look at things from one's own point of view. *From Mack's perspective, today's game would be an easy win.*

per·spi·ra·tion /pûr spə ˈrā shən/ n. the state of secreting sweat through the skin; sweat. *Perspiration is noticeable when players are actively engaged in a game.*

per·spire /pûr ˈspi ûr/ v. to secrete sweat through the skin. *The heat of the race caused many riders to perspire.*

per·suade /pûr ˈswād/ v. to convince by reasoning or pleading; to convince. *Trisha tried to persuade the referee to change his decision.*

phe·nom·e·nal /fi ˈno mə nəl/ adj. remarkable. *Zoe is a phenomenal ice-hockey goalie.*

paddling

photographer

pho·tog·ra·pher /fə ˈto grə fûr/ *n.* a person who practices or makes a business of taking pictures. *The photographer took some action shots of Keegan during the match.*

phys·i·cal /ˈfi zi kəl/ *adj.* involving a lot of bodily strength. *Motocross racing involves intense, physical demands.*

pleas·ant /ˈple zənt/ *adj.* agreeable; enjoyable. *It is always pleasant to spend time reading God's Word.*

poised /ˈpoizd/ *adj.* showing confidence and graciousness. *Was Chloe a poised, well-prepared rider?*

pop·u·lar·i·ty /po pyə ˈla rə tē/ *n.* the state of being popular. *The popularity of winter sports has risen in the last few years.*

po·si·tions /pə ˈzi shənz/ *n. pl.* plural of POSITION; the areas occupied by someone or something; locations. *Good hockey players are always in their correct positions.*

pos·ses·sion /pə ˈze shən/ *n.* a period of controlling the ball. *The rebound changed the possession of the basketball.*

post·ex·er·cise /pōst ˈek sûr siz/ *adj.* a routine after a workout. *A postexercise activity allows the body to cool down after exercising.*

post·op·er·a·tive /pōst ˈo pə rə tiv/ *adj.* after an operation. *Calvin received excellent postoperative care from the nurses.*

pos·ture /ˈpos chûr/ *n.* the position of the body. *Correct posture is important in fencing.*

po·ten·tial /pə ˈtent shəl/ *adj.* showing great promise. *Did the coach feel the team had a lot of potential ability?*

poul·try /ˈpōl trē/ *n.* domesticated birds such as chicken or turkey. *After the competition, contestants were served poultry for dinner.*

pretense

prac·tice /ˈprak təs/ *v.* the state of doing something repeatedly so as to become proficient or to improve. *Rex does train and practice his vaulting techniques six days a week.*

prac·ti·tion·ers /prak ˈti shə nûrz/ *n. pl.* plural of PRACTITIONER; those who practice an art or skill; experts. *Practitioners of martial arts are skilled in self-defense.*

praise·wor·thy /ˈprāz wûr thē/ *adj.* admirable; deserving praise. *Kaitlin's sportsmanlike and respectful behavior was praiseworthy.*

pre·cau·tion /pri ˈko shən/ *n.* caution or care taken beforehand. *Crash pads are used as a precaution to avoid injuries.*

pre·cise /pri ˈsis/ *adj.* exact. *The precise long-jump distance was twenty feet, seven inches.*

pres·ti·gious /pre ˈstē jəs/ *adj.* having prestige; honored. *Henri had a prestigious reputation for training Lipizzaners.*

pre·tense /ˈprē tents/ *n.* a claim made that is not supported by fact. *Nan joined the team on the pretense that she could water-ski.*

photographer

pret·zel /ˈpret səl/ *n.* derived from GERMAN; a slender, crisp or soft bread shaped like a stick or a knot, and usually salty. *Josie enjoyed a big soft pretzel as she watched the archers practice.*

prin·ci·pal /ˈprint sə pəl/ *n.* a person who has authority in a leading position. *The principal congratulated the team for its winning performance.*

prin·ci·ple /ˈprint sə pəl/ *n.* a rule of action or conduct. *Judges at a swim and diving meet must be people of principle.*

priv·i·lege /ˈpri və lij/ *n.* honor; pleasure. *Lorena had the privilege of praying for the golf team.*

pro·ac·tive /prō ˈak tiv/ *adj.* acting in anticipation toward future problems. *Carlota is proactive in living a healthy lifestyle.*

pro·ce·dure /prə ˈsē jûr/ *n.* method; way of doing things. *The team doctor followed the proper procedure to treat the injury.*

pro·fes·sion /prə ˈfe shən/ *n.* a calling or vocation; a career. *Few surfers are able to surf as a profession.*

pro·fes·sion·als /prə ˈfe shə nəlz/ *n. pl.* plural of PROFESSIONAL; people receiving a financial gain for their skills in sports. *A few tennis professionals have won all four major tennis tournaments.*

prog·ress /ˈpro grəs/ *n.* a development toward achieving a goal. *Kirsten made significant progress in the latest motocross race.*

pro·jec·tile /prə ˈjek ti əl/ *n.* an object that is thrown forward. *The discus is a disk-shaped projectile.*

pro·longed /prō ˈlȯngd/ *v.* past tense of PROLONG; to have lengthened the time to do something. *Art's broken ankle prolonged his inability to compete.*

pron·to /ˈpron tō/ *adv.* derived from SPANISH; without delay; fast. *The teacher instructed the class to line up for lunch, pronto.*

pro·pel /prə ˈpel/ *v.* to move forward by a force; drive. *Oars are used to propel a boat.*

prop·o·si·tion /pro pə ˈzi shən/ *n.* the state of something being placed or offered for consideration; proposal. *The coach's proposition to have a pizza party excited the archers.*

pro·pul·sion /prə ˈpul shən/ *n.* the state of driving something forward by force. *Javelin throwers use momentum as the propulsion for the javelin.*

pro·tect·ed /prə ˈtek təd/ *v.* past tense of PROTECT; to have covered beforehand; shielded. *All fencers must be protected by a fencing uniform.*

pum·per·nick·el /ˈpum pûr ni kəl/ *adj.* derived from GERMAN; a dark sourdough bread made with coarse rye flour. *Laura ordered a turkey sandwich with pumpernickel bread.*

qual·i·fied /ˈkwä lə fīd/ *v.* **1** past tense of QUALIFY; to have been made eligible. *The best teams qualified for the World Cup competition.* **2** modified. *Mrs. Davis qualified the rules during our meeting.*

qual·i·fy·ing /ˈkwä lə fī ing/ *v.* **1** to meet the requirements to advance in a competition. *Only two teams in our league will be qualifying to move up.* *adj.* **2** that which meets the requirements. *The players will play a qualifying round before the match.*

quar·ter·back /ˈkwȯr tûr bak/ *n.* the offensive back who calls and directs the plays. *Michelle plays quarterback for her flag football team.*

que·sa·dil·la /kä sə 'dē ə/ *n.* derived from SPANISH; a tortilla filled with cheese and other ingredients and grilled. *Eugene ate a quesadilla for a snack.*

qui·ver /'kwi vûr/ *n.* a long, narrow case for carrying or holding arrows. *Jackson placed ten arrows in the quiver.*

R

ran·dom /'ran dəm/ *adj.* lacking a definite pattern. *In a random sequence of errors, the home team scored three runs.*

rap·pel /rə 'pel/ *v.* to descend down a rope. *Thea began to slowly rappel to the ground.*

rau·cous /'rȯ kəs/ *adj.* loud; disorderly. *In a raucous voice, the coach objected to the umpire's call.*

rea·sons /'rē zənz/ *n. pl.* plural of REASON; sensible explanations. *There are good reasons for every rule in BMX racing.*

re·ceipt /ri 'sēt/ *n.* a written statement that something has been received. *Kyle took the receipt from the clerk when he paid for the skateboard.*

re·ceived /ri 'sēvd/ *v.* past tense of RECEIVE; to have taken something that was given, paid, or sent; accepted. *Have you received Jesus Christ as your Savior?*

rec·ol·lect /re kə 'lekt/ *v.* to remember. *I recollect the score from last year's final game.*

rec·om·mend /re kə 'mend/ *v.* to advise favorably. *Experts recommend that you warm up before playing football.*

rec·re·a·tion·al /re krē 'ā shə nəl/ *adj.* relating to relaxation; entertaining or fun. *Table tennis is a recreational activity in many countries.*

rect·an·gu·lar /rek 'tang gyə lûr/ *adj.* shaped like a rectangle; quadrilateral. *The sand court was rectangular and bordered by bleachers.*

ref·er·ee /re fə 'rē/ *n.* a sports official who governs play. *Did you know that there is only one referee in a soccer game?*

re·fine /ri 'fīn/ *v.* to improve or perfect again. *Coach David asked the team to refine their throwing techniques.*

re·fin·ish /rē 'fi nish/ *v.* the process of finishing again; redo. *Will Collette need to refinish her surfboard?*

re·flec·ted /ri 'flek təd/ *v.* **1** past tense of REFLECT; light bent back into one's eyes. *The sunlight reflected off the surface of the lake.* **2** to think about a past event. *Jonathan reflected on the enjoyment he had experienced at summer camp.*

re·flec·tive /ri 'flek tiv/ *adj.* having the ability to bend light back into one's eyes. *Owen wore a jacket with a reflective stripe down each sleeve.*

re·flex·es /'rē flek səz/ *n. pl.* plural of REFLEX; reactions or responses. *Garrison's reflexes were superb during the tournament.*

re·gen·er·ate /ri 'je nə rāt/ *v.* to make or produce again. *The retired archer will regenerate his skills by practicing.*

reg·u·la·tion /re gyə 'lā shən/ *adj.* relating to a rule dealing with details or procedures. *All players and coaches must wear regulation helmets on the ice.*

re·joined /ri 'joind/ *v.* past tense of REJOIN; to have joined again. *Cole rejoined his friends after attending his sister's soccer game.*

rel·e·vant /'re lə vənt/ *adj.* pertaining to the matter at hand. *Stan and Kaden enjoy talking about things relevant to boating.*

reluctant

re·luc·tant /ri ˈluk tənt/ *adj.* unwilling. *Tamara was reluctant to go white-water rafting.*

re·new·a·ble /ri ˈnoō ə bəl/ *adj.* capable of being replaced. *Permits to rock climb are renewable every year.*

re·pel /ri ˈpel/ *v.* to push, drive back, or exert an opposing force. *Geoff can repel the ball forcefully with his new racquet.*

re·po·si·tion /rē pə ˈzi shən/ *v.* to change the place of an item. *Did the placekicker need to reposition the ball?*

re·quire·ments /ri ˈkwī ûr mənts/ *n. pl.* plural of REQUIREMENT; regulations. *Our team follows the requirements for tournament play.*

req·ui·si·tion /re kwə ˈzi shən/ *n.* a state of seeking or requesting something that is required. *Principal Brady put in a requisition for new track-and-field equipment.*

re·sil·ient /ri ˈzil yənt/ *adj.* capable of recovering from misfortune. *After the canoe tipped over, resilient Gerron climbed right back in.*

re·sis·tance /ri ˈzis tənts/ *n.* an opposing or slowing force. *The water offered little resistance to the skier.*

res·o·lu·tion /re zə ˈloō shən/ *n.* state of being set free from something; determination. *A shoot-out is the resolution to a tied game in ice hockey.*

re·solved /ri ˈzolvd/ *v.* past tense of RESOLVE; to have determined, solved, or settled. *The arguing teammates resolved to put aside their differences.*

re·sound·ing /ri ˈzoun ding/ *adj.* resonating; echoing. *With resounding joy, Eloise sang a worship song of praise.*

re·spect·a·ble /ri ˈspek tə bəl/ *adj.* capable of being viewed favorably. *It is important to demonstrate respectable conduct at all times.*

reversed

re·spec·ted /ri ˈspek təd/ *v.* past tense of RESPECT; esteemed. *Professional athletes are respected when they make wise choices.*

res·pi·ra·tion /res pə ˈrā shən/ *n.* the state of breathing. *One's respiration will increase when aggressively involved in a sport.*

re·spon·si·bil·i·ty /ri spont sə ˈbi lə tē/ *n.* reliability; state of being responsible. *Christian athletes have the responsibility to share Christ's love.*

res·tau·rant /ˈres tə ränt/ *n.* a business establishment where meals or refreshments can be purchased. *Wyatt and Alexa ate lunch at the club restaurant after their golf game.*

ret·ro·spect /ˈre trə spekt/ *n.* to look back and examine or remember events; a recollection. *In retrospect, the long-jump event ran smoothly and was a success.*

re·ver·ber·ate /ri ˈvûr bə rāt/ *v.* to echo repeatedly. *The impact of the ball did reverberate loudly in the enclosed court.*

re·vered /ri ˈvîrd/ *v.* past tense of REVERE; admired; respected. *Jesus should be highly revered for His great love toward us.*

re·versed /ri ˈvûrsd/ *v.* past tense of REVERSE; to have turned something to the opposite direction, order, or position. *Due to the weather, the judges reversed the order of race events.*

restaurant

re·vived /ri 'vivd/ v. past tense of REVIVE; brought back to life. *Water revived the dehydrated runner.*

rhy·thm /'ri thəm/ n. a movement with a recurring pattern of elements; repetition. *It is important to have rhythm when paddling a kayak.*

rhyth·mic /'rith mik/ adj. having a rhythm. *Are many of the movements in martial arts rhythmic?*

ric·o·chet /'ri kə shā/ v. to hit a surface and bounce back; rebound. *The rubber ball will quickly ricochet off the court walls.*

ro·ta·tion /rō 'tā shən/ n. a turn around an axis. *I could tell that the wheel was bent from its wobbly rotation.*

ro·tun·da /rō 'tun də/ n. derived from ITALIAN; a round building often covered by a dome. *The ceiling of the rotunda had beautiful paintings of horses.*

rough·hous·ing /'ruf hou zing/ v. behaving in a rough, boisterous manner. *Two players were roughhousing and put into the penalty box.*

route /'rōōt/ n. a path; a course. *Martin carved a route in the fresh snow as he descended the mountain.*

S

sat·el·lite /'sa tə lit/ n. a device put into orbit around Earth or another planet to relay information or transmit communications signals. *Billions of people received the World Cup broadcast via satellite.*

sau·er·kraut /'sou ûr krout/ n. derived from GERMAN; shredded cabbage fermented in its own juice with salt. *Phillip ordered sauerkraut and sausage from the menu.*

sched·ules /'ske jəlz/ n. pl. plural of SCHEDULE; lists of commitments or appointments; plans. *The coach checked all of the time schedules before the big meet.*

schol·ar·ship /'sko lûr ship/ n. a state of awarding money; money given to help a worthy student continue his or her educational studies; a grant. *Lois received a full athletic scholarship to her college of choice.*

scrim·mage /'skri mij/ n. practice play. *Our offensive and defensive teams practice during a scrimmage.*

scul·ling /'sku ling/ n. a form of rowing; scull racing. *Sculling is a type of rowing that does not have a navigator.*

sed·en·tar·y /'se dən târ ē/ adj. inclined to sit; inactive. *Everyone should live an active lifestyle and not be sedentary.*

seize /'sēz/ v. to take possession of; to take hold of suddenly; grab. *The team is working diligently to seize the championship this year.*

se·lec·tion /sə 'lek shən/ n. the state of gathering or choosing something from among others. *There was a large selection of ski apparel to purchase.*

selt·zer /'selt sûr/ n. derived from GERMAN; artificially carbonated water. *Seltzer is used in carbonated beverages such as soda pop.*

sem·i·final /se mē 'fi nəl/ adj. the last round before the ending match of a competition. *Mason sprained his ankle during the semifinal match.*

rotunda

senior   **spherical**

se·nior /'sē nyûr/ *adj.* leading; superior; higher ranking. *Franklin is a senior member of the volleyball team.*

sense /'sents/ *n.* **1** a function of perception such as sight, hearing, touch, smell, or taste. *April used her sense of hearing to tell when to shift the gears.* *v.* **2** to become conscious of. *Perhaps you can sense when the Lord is leading you.*

sep·a·rat·ed /'se pə rā təd/ *v.* past tense of SEPARATE; divided. *A tall net separated the two volleyball teams.*

sep·a·rate·ly /'se pə rət lē/ *adv.* distinctly; on their own. *Bryce and Reggie arrived separately for the golf tournament.*

sig·nif·i·cant /sig 'ni fi kənt/ *adj.* important. *Wearing a life vest is significant to one's safety on a boat.*

sim·u·lat·ed /'sim yə lā təd/ *v.* past tense of SIMULATE; to have replicated the effect or features of something. *The computerized game effectively simulated motocross events.*

si·mul·ta·ne·ous·ly /sī məl 'tā nē əs lē/ *adv.* occurring at the same time as something else. *All the runners began racing simultaneously.*

since /'sints/ *adv.* **1** from a definite time in the past until now. *Neal learned to water-ski as a boy, and he has loved it ever since.* *conj.* **2** because. *Since Isaac was not paying attention, he fell from the boat.*

sin·cere·ly /sin 'sîr lē/ *adv.* genuinely; truly. *Paloma was sincerely honored when named golf team captain.*

sla·lom /'slä ləm/ *n.* a timed race over a zigzag course. *Hannah entered the competition for the women's giant slalom.*

so·cia·ble /'sō shə bəl/ *adj.* able to seek out the company of other people or engage in social interaction; friendly; outgoing. *The sport of golf allows participants to be sociable with fellow players.*

so·ci·e·ty /sə 'sī ə tē/ *n.* a state of companionship; a group of people, generally with a common interest or role. *Angela gives back to society by teaching children how to play golf.*

som·bre·ro /səm 'brâr ō/ *n.* derived from SPANISH; a high crowned hat with a very wide brim. *The wide brim of a sombrero shaded Hector's face from the sun.*

sought /'sȯt/ *v.* past tense of SEEK; looked for. *Nick eagerly sought the results of the men's big air competition.*

sou·ve·nir /'sōō və nîr/ *n.* a keepsake. *Charley bought a souvenir after the track-and-field finals.*

sov·er·eign /'so və rən/ *n.* above all others; supreme; greatest. *Our God is loving, just, and sovereign.*

spa·ghet·ti /spə 'ge tē/ *n.* derived from ITALIAN; long, thin strips of pasta. *A plate of spaghetti was a welcome sight to the hungry riders.*

spe·cial·ize /'spe shə līz/ *v.* making a concentrated study in one kind of activity. *Ravinder hopes to specialize in New Testament history.*

spe·cial·ty /'spe shəl tē/ *n.* a state of expertise in one kind of activity. *Hong Choi's specialty is tae kwon do.*

spec·ta·tor /'spek tā tûr/ *n.* one who watches. *Being a spectator is not as much fun as playing in a baseball game.*

spher·i·cal /'sfîr i kəl/ *adj.* shaped like a sphere; round. *The inflated, spherical volleyball was white and black.*

sports·man·ship /ˈspôrts mən ship/ *n.* a quality of fair conduct; fair behavior during participation in a sport. *Brody displayed great sportsmanship during the pole-vault competition.*

spring·board /ˈspring bôrd/ *n.* a flexible board secured at one end for diving. *A diver can dive off of a springboard or platform.*

sprint·er /ˈsprin tûr/ *n.* one who sprints; a short-distance runner. *Eric Liddell was a Christian missionary as well as a sprinter.*

sta·di·um /ˈstā dē əm/ *n.* a venue for spectators at sporting events. *Will the new stadium be completed before the track meet?*

stam·i·na /ˈsta mə nə/ *n.* endurance. *Daily workouts build one's stamina.*

sta·tion·ar·y /ˈstā shə när ē/ *adj.* immobile. *A diving board is stationary since it is bolted to the concrete.*

sta·tion·er·y /ˈstā shə när ē/ *n.* materials used for writing such as paper, pens, and envelopes. *The captain used stationery to write thank-you notes to the team.*

sta·tis·ti·cal·ly /stə ˈtis ti kə lē/ *adv.* having the characteristic of informative pieces; precisely. *The history of track-and-field events statistically shows Greek origins.*

sta·tis·tics /stə ˈtis tiks/ *n. pl.* plural of STATISTIC; a collection of data. *Kim's statistics are so impressive that scouts are watching her.*

sta·tus /ˈstā təs/ *n.* position in relation to others. *A softball player's status depends on his or her performance.*

stop·pa·ges /ˈsto pi jəz/ *n. pl.* plural of STOPPAGE; the act of stopping; obstructions. *Too much fighting leads to many stoppages during a game.*

stor·age /ˈstôr ij/ *n.* a place of safekeeping; a space in which items are placed for safekeeping and storing. *Cyril was asked to take the vaulting poles out of storage.*

strat·e·giz·ing /ˈstra tə ji zing/ *v.* devising a plan. *Antoni is strategizing ways to improve his running time.*

strat·e·gy /ˈstra tə jē/ *n.* a careful plan or method. *Strategy and skill are vital to playing basketball.*

strik·ers /ˈstri kûrz/ *n. pl.* plural of STRIKER; players on a soccer team whose main responsibility is to score goals. *Tammy warmed up by stretching with other strikers on the team.*

strokes /ˈstrōks/ *n. pl.* plural of STROKE; unbroken movements. *Strokes used in rowing consist of recovery, catch, drive, and release.*

stru·del /ˈstroo dəl/ *n.* derived from GERMAN; a rolled pastry made from thin dough that contains a filling. *Sunny ate a cherry strudel for dessert.*

sub·jec·tion /səb ˈjek shən/ *n.* the state of bringing under control. *The weight of a javelin is in subjection to federation rules.*

sub·scrip·tion /səb ˈskrip shən/ *n.* the state of agreement to sign for something and pay for it. *Jesse renewed his sport's magazine subscription last week.*

sub·stan·tial /səb ˈstant shəl/ *adj.* ample. *We had substantial time to practice our surfing skills.*

sub·sti·tute /ˈsub stə toot/ *adj.* **1** temporary replacement. *Was Theo the only substitute player for the team in last week's game?* *n.* **2** a replacement. *Having only one substitute for the match, the players pushed through the game.*

sub·to·tal /ˈsub tō təl/ *n.* the sum of a partial set of figures. *The subtotal came to fifty-five dollars, before tax.*

successful

suc·cess·ful /sək ˈses fəl/ *adj.* favorable; effective. *The European team played a successful tournament and won the title.*

suc·ces·sion /sək ˈse shən/ *n.* a sequence. *A volleyball player is not allowed to hit the ball twice in succession.*

suf·fi·cient /sə ˈfi shənt/ *adj.* enough. *Players who do not drink sufficient water risk dehydration.*

su·per·ath·lete /ˈsoo pûr ath lēt/ *n.* an athlete with more skills and abilities than other athletes. *A superathlete has the ability to play several sports well.*

su·per·ef·fec·tive /ˈsoo pûr i fek tiv/ *adj.* better results than anticipated. *The coach's supereffective techniques assist the cross-country team.*

su·per·fi·cial /soo pûr ˈfi shəl/ *adj.* on the surface; not deep. *Shawn's board received a superficial scratch.*

su·per·sede /soo pûr ˈsēd/ *v.* to replace with higher qualities. *Newer boat designs supersede older models.*

sup·pos·ing /sə ˈpō zing/ *v.* to continually put one's thoughts under an assumption. *Hallie is supposing she will do well since she has trained hard.*

surf·boards /ˈsûrf bôrdz/ *n. pl.* plural of SURFBOARD; more than one surfboard. *Ten surfboards were stuck in the sand.*

sur·passed /sûr ˈpasd/ *v.* past tense of SURPASS; exceeded; to have gone beyond. *Have you surpassed a previous personal running record?*

swim·ming pool /ˈswi ming pool/ *n.* a structure filled with water for recreational or competitive use. *Jennifer jumped into the swimming pool and began to warm up.*

tension

T

tac·tics /ˈtak tiks/ *n. pl.* plural of TACTIC; methods used in combat. *Do all fencing clubs teach the same tactics?*

taut /ˈtôt/ *adj.* having no slack; stretched tightly. *The bowstring must be taut before the arrow is released.*

tech·ni·cal /ˈtek ni kəl/ *adj.* relating to a specific subject. *A technical foul was called for poor sportsmanship.*

tech·nique /tek ˈnēk/ *n.* a method. *In-line skaters and skateboarders develop their own technique.*

tech·nol·o·gy /tek ˈno lə jē/ *n.* application and method of applying technical knowledge. *Modern engineering technology enables motorcycles to run faster.*

tel·e·vised /ˈte lə vizd/ *v.* past tense of TELEVISE; to have broadcasted a far distance to be seen. *The final match was televised to millions of viewers.*

tel·e·vi·sion /ˈte lə vi zhən/ *n.* an electronic device that receives and projects pictures and sounds. *Vance watched the World Championship on the television.*

ten·sion /ˈtent shən/ *n.* the act of being stretched to stiffness; tautness. *The tension of the bow propelled the arrow toward the target.*

surfboards

ter·i·ya·ki /tär ē 'yä kē/ *adj.* derived from JAPANESE; a dish of meat or fish marinated in a seasoned soy sauce marinade. *Anjali loves teriyaki beef over rice.*

ter·rain /tə 'rān/ *n.* landscape; ground. *Jerome felt confident as he raced along the bumpy terrain.*

ther·mo·gen·ic /thûr mə 'je nik/ *adj.* relating to the production of heat. *A thermogenic sport, such as tennis, raises one's body temperature.*

ther·mog·ra·phy /thûr 'mo grə fē/ *n.* a process of printing or writing using heat. *Thermography is a printing process that produces raised images.*

ther·mom·e·ter /thûr 'mo mə tûr/ *n.* a device to measure heat. *The outdoor thermometer read 98 degrees Fahrenheit.*

ther·mo·stat /'thûr mə stat/ *n.* a device that automatically regulates heat. *The thermostat at the indoor tennis club read 68 degrees Fahrenheit.*

thor·ough·ly /'thûr ō lē/ *adv.* done fully. *Justin thoroughly practiced before the finals competition.*

though /'thō/ *conj.* even if; although. *Though it was snowing, the Alpine events continued.*

thought·less·ly /'thòt ləs lē/ *adv.* carelessly. *The ski jumper thoughtlessly broke form and landed awkwardly.*

through·out /thrōō 'out/ *prep.* during the whole time. *Dimitri had a positive attitude throughout the competition.*

tie·break·er /'tī brā kûr/ *n.* a method used to decide the winner of a competition with a tied score. *Grace won the tiebreaker after scoring the final point.*

ti·ta·ni·um /tī 'tā nē əm/ *n.* a strong, lightweight, metallic element. *Brenda's new golf clubs were made of titanium.*

torque /'tôrk/ *n.* a rotating force that causes turning and twisting. *During a golf swing, torque is a twisting movement of the club's shaft.*

tor·so /'tôr sō/ *n.* the upper part of the body, not including the head and the arms. *Felipe touched Hunter's torso with his blade and scored a point.*

tor·til·la /tôr 'tē ə/ *n.* derived from SPANISH; a round, thin bread made from cornmeal or wheat flour. *Juan asked for one more tortilla to eat with his fajitas.*

touch·down /'tuch doun/ *n.* a score of six points in American football. *The Mountain Goats scored a touchdown!*

tour·na·ment /'toor nə mənt/ *n.* a series of games. *The soccer tournament began with a parade of athletes.*

tow·rope /'tō rōp/ *n.* a line used in towing a water-skier behind a boat; a line used for towing. *The beginning water-skier gripped the towrope tightly.*

trac·tion /'trak shən/ *n.* adhesive friction that causes a thing to hold firmly to a surface; grip. *It is difficult for wheels to have traction on wet surfaces.*

tra·jec·to·ry /trə 'jek tə rē/ *n.* the path or route of a flying object. *The golf ball's trajectory determines how far it goes down the fairway.*

titanium

transitional

tran·si·tion·al /tran ˈzi shə nəl/ *adj.* moves from one stage to another. *Is this a transitional period for the Paralympics?*

trans·par·en·cy /trants ˈpâr ənt sē/ *n.* the quality of light passing through objects so they can be seen from one side to the other side. *The transparency of the water allowed Seth to see the sunken rings.*

trans·verse /tranz ˈvûrs/ *adj.* extending across; horizontal. *Lee's body dislodged the transverse crossbar during his high jump.*

tra·versed /trə ˈvûrsd/ *v.* past tense of TRAVERSE; to have traveled across, over, or through a particular location. *Meika successfully traversed the course during the women's event.*

tre·men·dous /tri ˈmen dəs/ *adj.* incredible. *Tremendous applause erupted after the record-breaking jump.*

trep·i·da·tion /tre pə ˈdā shən/ *n.* fear. *I approached my first surfing lesson with much trepidation.*

triv·i·a /ˈtri vē ə/ *n. pl.* unimportant information or details. *Do you know any trivia about baseball?*

U

un·au·tho·rized /ˈun ȯ thə rīzd/ *adj.* not warranted by proper authority; not duly commissioned. *Climbers should always avoid wandering into unauthorized areas.*

un·con·vinced /ən kən ˈvinst/ *adj.* doubtful. *We were unconvinced that the scoreboard was accurate.*

un·der·es·ti·mate /ən dûr ˈes tə māt/ *v.* to estimate less than the actual size or amount. *People should never underestimate the power of prayer.*

visor

un·der·nour·ished /ən dûr ˈnûr isht/ *adj.* having less than the minimum amount of food for proper nourishment. *The athlete volunteered his time to help undernourished children.*

un·fin·ished /ən ˈfi nisht/ *adj.* not yet at an end; incomplete. *Phil's surfboard is still in the garage because it is unfinished.*

u·ni·fy /ˈyo͞o nə fī/ *v.* to unite. *Working together will unify the team.*

un·nec·es·sar·y /ən ˈne sə sâr ē/ *adj.* needless. *Violet was told that her entry fee payment was unnecessary.*

V

vault·ed /ˈvȯl təd/ *v.* past tense of VAULT; to have executed a leap with the aid of the hands or a pole. *Janelle successfully vaulted over the high crossbar.*

ve·loc·i·ty /və ˈlo sə tē/ *n.* speed. *The velocity of a tennis serve can be over one hundred miles per hour.*

ve·ran·da /və ˈran də/ *n.* derived from HINDI; a roofed portico attached to the exterior of a building; a covered patio. *The veranda was the coolest place to be on a hot summer night.*

ver·sa·tile /ˈvûr sə təl/ *adj.* easily turning from one thing to another; changeable. *A versatile player is very good at batting and also at fielding.*

ver·sions /ˈvûr zhənz/ *n. pl.* plural of VERSION; forms or types of. *Different versions of water polo can involve variations in play area.*

ver·ti·cal /ˈvûr ti kəl/ *adj.* upright at a right angle to the horizon. *Vertical posts hold a crossbar during pole-vault or high-jump events.*

vi·sor /ˈvī zûr/ *n.* the upper, front piece of a helmet. *Renee's visor shields her eyes from the sun.*

vi·su·al /ˈvi zhə wəl/ *adj.* relating to vision. *Coach Wright used the whiteboard as a visual aid to explain the play.*

vi·va·cious /vi ˈvā shəs/ *adj.* having the quality of liveliness; perky; lively. *Does Stephanie have a vivacious personality?*

vol·leyed /ˈvo lēd/ *v.* past tense of VOLLEY; to have hit a ball or shuttlecock in succession without allowing it to hit the ground. *In badminton, the shuttlecock is always volleyed over the net.*

wa·ter·line /ˈwȯ tûr lin/ *n.* a line to which a body of water rises. *The floating water-polo nets touched the waterline in the pool.*

weird /ˈwîrd/ *adj.* odd; unusual; strange. *Many skateboards have weird designs on their decks.*

well-con·di·tioned /wel kən ˈdi shənd/ *adj.* being in good physical condition or shape. *The well-conditioned athlete effortlessly swam laps.*

wide·spread /ˈwid spred/ *adj.* happening in many places; prevalent. *After a major win, the news of the team's success was widespread.*